Bennett's Small House Catalog 1920

Ray H. Bennett Lumber Co., Inc.

Dover Publications, Inc.
New York

Published in Canada by General Publishing Company, Ltd., 30 Lesmill Road, Don Mills, Toronto, Ontario.

Published in the United Kingdom by Constable and Company, Ltd., 3 The Lanchesters, 162–164 Fulham Palace Road, London W6 9ER.

Bibliographical Note

This Dover edition, first published in 1993, is an unabridged republication of *Bennett Homes: Better-Built Ready-Cut*, Catalog No. 18, published by Ray H. Bennett Lumber Co., Inc., North Tonawanda, N.Y., in 1920. The Dover edition also includes three individual enclosures: a company letter, price list and order form. The original front and back covers of the catalog were printed in three colors.

Library of Congress Cataloging-in-Publication Data

Bennett's small house catalog, 1920 / Ray H. Bennett Lumber Co., Inc.
      p.   cm.
   "An unabridged republication of Bennett homes: better-built ready-cut, catalog no. 18, published by Ray H. Bennett Lumber Co., Inc., North Tonawanda, N.Y., in 1920."
   ISBN 0-486-27809-3
   1. Small houses—United States—Designs and plans—Catalogs. I. Ray H. Bennett Lumber Co., Inc. II. Dover Publications, Inc. III. Bennett homes. IV. Title: Small house catalog, 1920.
NA7205.B43   1993
728'.37'0222—dc20   93-40012
                                             CIP

Manufactured in the United States of America
Dover Publications, Inc., 31 East 2nd Street, Mineola, N.Y. 11501

Bennett Homes

Better-Built — Ready-Cut

Ray H. Bennett Lumber Co., Inc.
NORTH TONAWANDA - N.Y.

[Original front cover]

Bennett Homes
Better Built Ready Cut

RAY H. BENNETT LUMBER CO., Inc.

**LUMBER
LATH - SHINGLES
WINDOWS - DOORS
MILL WORK**

NORTH TONAWANDA, N.Y.

Dear Friend,

We send this catalog to you with just one thought in mind,
Service. As you turn the pages and study the various houses,
remember that we are planning and building for YOU. No trouble
is too great, no detail too small, if by personal consideration
and supervision we can provide you with your ideal home.

Our architects have studied the requirement of comfortable,
convenient, up-to-date houses. In the designs shown in this
catalog, you will find embodied their ideas — the results of
considering the greatest convenience at the least cost.

Not only do we supply you with blue prints of the house you
select, but our special service department is ready to assist
you in your interior decorating. Then too, our service
department can give you any information you require in regard
to the erection of your house.

You naturally will want to know the approximate cost of erect-
ing the house of your choice, the cost of the mason work,
plumbing, lighting, heating, etc. This we shall be glad to
furnish you, if you will write to us for such information.

In buying a Bennett Home, you are really gratifying your individual tastes. You have infinite choice of designs, any of
which can be slightly or moderately altered. You can choose
your own color for outside paint and inside finish. Cupboards
and closets of convenient size and situation, bay windows,
French doors, fire places, stairways, colonnades, — all these
are yours to command.

We have already selected for you the best framing materials,
lumber and hardware. The little touches that make the home and
radiate the personality of the owners — these we leave to your
individual choice.

It is YOUR home that you are to build, and we offer you our
assistance and co-operation.

                    Cordially Yours,

JAS|RN   RAY H. BENNETT LUMBER CO., INC.

Bennett Homes
Better-Built — Ready-Cut

PRICES OF BENNETT HOMES
DECEMBER 1, 1921

PRICES ARE NET F. O. B. CARS NORTH TONAWANDA, N. Y.
DELIVERED PRICES QUOTED ON REQUEST.
TERMS: Net Cash with Order.

TERMS:

1. **Cash with Order.** 5% discount from gross amount allowed when Cash in full is sent with order, **or**
2. **25% Cash with Order.** Balance sight draft with order bill of lading attached.
   No discount from gross amount allowed under these terms.

WE GUARANTEE SATISFACTION OR MONEY BACK.

Name	Page	Gross	5% Cash Discount	Net
Aberdeen, Plan A	30	$1944.78	$ 97.23	$1847.55
Aberdeen, Plan B	30	2418.89	120.94	2297.95
Arcadia, Plan A	31	1610.33	80.51	1529.82
Arcadia, Plan B	31	1907.57	95.37	1812.20
Atherton	32	2481.17	124.05	2357.12
Auburn, Plan A	56	1074.09	53.70	1020.39
Auburn, Plan B	56	1273.94	63.69	1210.25
Avon	10	2940.28	147.00	2793.28
Beverly, Plan A	60	1142.60	57.13	1085.47
Beverly, Plan B	60	1224.00	61.20	1162.80
Bison	22	2342.62	117.13	2225.49
Bryant	12	2465.12	123.25	2341.87
Charlotte, Plan B	11	3184.52	159.22	3025.30
Clarendon	39	3345.17	167.25	3177.92
Cleo	26	2313.83	115.69	2198.14
Cloverdale, Plan A	55	1380.97	69.04	1311.93
Cloverdale, Plan B	55	1519.36	75.96	1443.40
Concord, Reg.	61	1317.45	65.87	1251.58
Concord, Plan B	61	1585.31	79.26	1506.05
Colonial	44	4243.05	212.15	4030.90
Delaware, Plan A	58	1747.45	87.37	1660.08
Delaware, Plan B	58	1949.84	97.49	1852.35
Dover, Reg.	50	2120.89	106.04	2014.85
Dover, Plan B	50	2275.89	113.79	2162.10
Emerson	62	1697.23	84.86	1612.37
Erie	45	2281.00	114.05	2166.95
Flanders	35	2024.85	101.24	1923.61
Forsyth	38	3049.37	152.46	2896.91
Franklin	17	2550.71	127.53	2423.18
Frederick	46	3669.70	183.48	3486.22
Fulton	25	2552.78	127.63	2425.15
Genesee	41	2202.63	110.13	2092.50
Hamilton	24	2994.63	149.73	2844.90
Harriet	33	2776.88	138.84	2638.04
Hartley	43	2753.12	137.65	2615.47
Harvard	14	2071.13	103.55	1967.58
Ideal	23	2654.70	132.73	2521.97
Ilion	13	2440.36	122.01	2318.35
Janis	40	3088.00	154.40	2933.60
Kenmore, Plan A	54	804.91	40.24	764.67
Kenmore, Plan B	54	1039.82	51.99	987.83
Lancaster	34	2905.94	145.29	2760.65
La Salle	21	3076.84	153.84	2923.00
Lawton, Plan A	53	1647.97	82.39	1565.58
Lawton, Plan B	53	1825.67	91.28	1734.39
Lincoln	16	2849.67	142.48	2707.19

Name	Page	Gross	5% Cash Discount	Net
Madison	66	$2510.10	$125.50	$2384.60
Maidstone, Plan A	52	1131.47	56.57	1074.90
Maidstone, Plan B	52	1386.96	69.34	1317.62
Monroe	59	2100.69	105.03	1995.66
Nelson	47	1728.63	86.43	1642.20
New Hartford	19	2185.30	109.26	2076.04
Niagara	20	2459.91	122.99	2336.92
Olean	42	2012.08	100.60	1911.48
Ontario	64	2051.56	102.57	1948.99
Potomac	18	3124.68	156.23	2968.45
Raymond	15	2305.83	115.29	2190.54
Richard	48	2045.57	102.27	1943.30
Rochester	49	2340.15	117.00	2223.15
Salem	28	2538.93	126.94	2411.99
Shamrock, Plan A	57	1124.27	56.21	1068.06
Shamrock, Plan B	57	1429.11	71.45	1357.66
Sherrill, Plan A	51	1551.68	77.58	1474.10
Sherrill, Plan B	51	1898.22	94.91	1803.31
Stanley	65	1230.88	61.54	1169.34
Tremont	67	4051.07	202.55	3848.52
Waverly	63	2006.09	100.30	1905.79
Woodward	29	1723.77	86.18	1637.59
York	27	1914.00	95.60	1818.40

SUMMER COTTAGES, Pages 68-69

Name	Page	Gross	5% Cash Discount	Net
Wenona	68	$842.07	$42.10	$799.97
Newport	68	786.86	39.34	747.52
Ivernia	69	702.34	35.11	667.23
Linwood	69	800.36	40.01	760.35

GARAGES, Pages 69-70

Name	Size	Gross	5% Cash Discount	Net
Buick	10 x 14	$170.12	$ 8.50	$161.62
Buick	10 x 16	182.48	9.12	173.36
Buick	12 x 16	196.45	9.82	186.63
Buick	12 x 18	210.21	10.51	199.70
Buick	12 x 20	217.08	10.85	206.23
Cadillac	18 x 16	275.84	13.79	262.05
Cadillac	18 x 18	293.09	14.65	278.44
Cadillac	18 x 20	306.98	15.34	291.64
Cadillac	20 x 18	306.98	15.34	291.64
Cadillac	20 x 20	325.52	16.27	309.25
Cadillac	27 x 20	417.76	20.88	396.88
Hudson	10 x 14	169.83	8.49	161.34
Hudson	10 x 16	181.72	9.08	172.64
Hudson	12 x 16	199.97	9.99	189.98
Hudson	12 x 18	208.73	10.43	198.30
Hudson	14 x 16	212.73	10.63	202.10
Hudson	14 x 18	226.63	10.33	215.30
Peerless	18 x 16	288.10	14.40	273.70
Peerless	18 x 18	301.76	15.08	286.68
Peerless	18 x 20	315.26	15.76	299.50
Peerless	20 x 18	315.26	15.76	299.50
Peerless	20 x 20	327.42	16.37	311.05
Bennett Special	8 x 12	90.94	4.54	86.40
Bennett Special	8 x 14	97.61	4.88	92.73
Bennett Special	8 x 16	110.18	5.50	104.68
Bennett Special	10 x 12	99.22	4.96	94.26
Bennett Special	10 x 14	109.25	5.46	103.79
Bennett Special	10 x 16	122.23	6.11	116.12

Ray H. Bennett Lumber Co., Inc.
NORTH TONAWANDA — N.Y.

Bennett Homes
Better-Built Ready-Cut

ORDER FORM

To RAY H. BENNETT LUMBER CO., Inc.

North Tonawanda, N. Y.

Date...

Gentlemen:

I enclose..for $.........................for which you agree to ship

Draft, Money Order, Certified Check, or Currency

me at once the home described in your Catalog as ....and as found on page.......... The amount I am send-

ing is {full {part -payment for the complete house and any extras or changes as noted below.

....

Name as you regularly sign it.

....

STREET and NUMBER, or other ADDRESS   TOWN or CITY

....

COUNTY   STATE

SHIPPING INSTRUCTIONS—Print or write very plainly to avoid error

Ship to (NAME)..

Where {STREET NO. {or R. D. ROUTE}.. TOWN or CITY...........................

(COUNTY)..STATE.........................

Is there a freight station and agent?.................................RAILROAD.........................

REMARKS:..

....

....

....

[Use back of this form for additional remarks or notes]

My selection of paint colors is:

for body of house....................................No.........   for porch floor...............................No.......

for outside trim....................................No.........   for porch ceiling.............................No.......

for inside trim....................................No.........   For bathrooms we furnish white enamel finish unless you particularly specify other paint or varnish.

WE GUARANTEE ENTIRE SATISFACTION OR MONEY BACK

We guarantee to furnish all the lumber, lath, shingles, finishing lumber, doors, windows, frames, floor and interior trim, hardware, nails, tinware, paints, stains, varnishes of sufficient quantity and equal to or better than the grades specified to complete the house according to the plan, and specifications given in Catalog. We further guarantee that there will be no extras, and that all material will reach you in perfect condition. Should any shortage occur we agree to replace the material either by shipping the necessary material or paying you whatever it costs to buy it locally.

RAY H. BENNETT LUMBER CO., Inc.

THIS book is the story, in word and picture, of actual homes proven by living people to be Beautiful, Practical, Substantial. ¶ The designs and plans are the final creations, after years of study and experience, of Foremost American Authorities on Home Architecture and Construction. ¶ Economy is the controlling thought in these plans—not economy that merely cheapens but that which eliminates all unnecessary costs without sacrifice of appearance, strength or utility. ¶ Bennett Homes are truly Better-Built—better to look at, better to live in and better to last.

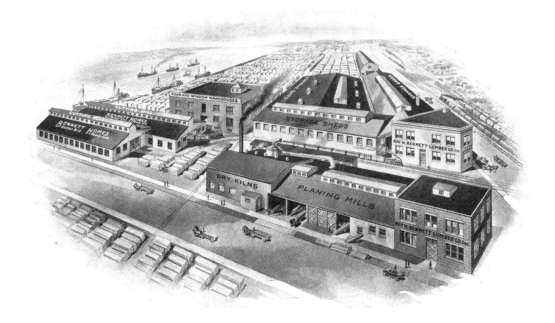

CATALOG No. 18

Copyright 1920 by

Ray H. Bennett Lumber Co., Inc.
NORTH TONAWANDA - N.Y.

ESTABLISHED 1902

INDEX

REFERENCES

THE STATE NATIONAL BANK
NORTH TONAWANDA, N. Y.

BUFFALO TRUST COMPANY
BUFFALO, N. Y.

THE FIRST TRUST CO. OF
TONAWANDA
TONAWANDA, N. Y.

REFERENCES

OUR CUSTOMERS EVERYWHERE
ANY BANK OR TRUST COMPANY
DUN'S, BRADSTREET'S OR OTHER
COMMERCIAL AGENCIES.

"Home-keeping hearts are happiest;
For those who wander they know not where
Are full of trouble and full of care;
To stay at home is best."
—LONGFELLOW

The first home was purposely built beside the "Sacred Fire".

The story runs that fire came as a gift from the Gods to Man. And so heavenly seemed its qualities of beauty, light and warmth, that Man reverenced it—ceased wandering and built his abode around its glowing radiance.

Through the ages—from the rugged cave, the rough tent of animal skins, the crude log cabin, down to the Home Beautiful of To-day—home building has been the strong primal instinct. Men have practiced all the pursuits of peace and war for those things for which home stands—love, family, hospitality, security, worship. Indeed, the home building spirit is the very backbone of civilization. Intelligent, thoughtful men always desire their families to live the home life, because they know that the best of physical, mental and moral powers are developed under home's benign influence.

Almost the first thought of the Pilgrims after they had landed on America's new shores was of a home. And so immediately they built themselves sturdy houses of the straight-shafted pine trees that stood everywhere about the rugged shores. And some of these homes are still standing, amazing testimony to the vigor and endurance of wood.

Today, more than ever before, people are seriously considering how they shall live. They realize that the dwelling place has a marked influence upon living and character—that the inspiration of home, next to religion, is the greatest in life.

Perforce, many must live part of their lives in the rented house. But however desirable, no family can ever acquire quite that deep-seated love and interest for, nor have the incentive to adorn and beautify, a dwelling place for which they pay toll to a landlord. But when the place which shelters the family belongs to them, when they know that every thought and every dollar they put into it is a permanent investment which pays big dividends in the family happiness and contentment—then that place, however lowly or humble, becomes truly a home. Naturally then, the tendency is strongly toward the owned private home.

The dainty cottage—the inviting semi-bungalow—the comfortable Colonial—the cosy story-and-a-half—these are the leading types of homes to-day. And when there is built into them that particular beauty, and those conveniences—modern sanitation, lighting, ventilation and heating—that will suit the taste of the individual family, their mode of living and their pocketbook—then indeed does the dwelling place become "a thing of beauty and a joy forever".

Bennett Homes, Better-Built and Ready-Cut, satisfy every desire and every need of home-lovers—for the dwelling-place which shall possess charm, convenience and endurance to the greatest extent consistent with the desired investment.

A Better-Built idea—routing (instead of cleating) stair-stringers for fine workmanship, and accurate fit.

HOW SCIENCE SOLVED THE HIGH COST OF HOME-BUILDING

Up to the present, the great drawback to home-building has been the excessive cost, by the individually-built-house method.

Plans by experienced architects have been costly; the cost of lumber has been high; the amount of labor necessary to cut and trim rough and finished lumber has been a serious item; there have been endless worries—delays—extra costs; plans have looked good on paper, but have not worked out well; contractors have been known to be careless about the quality of the material and of the work on the job.

What will avoid all the usual waste, delays, disappointments, and—what will cut the cost of building a home? Science says—*"simplify"*—*standardize"*—*"eliminate waste."*

"This is the day of brains that plans for thousands at a time, instead of one. Why is it necessary to plan every individual home that is built? There's a wiser, more economical way. Once the plan for a house has been tried and proven true, use it many times over; let hundreds of people divide the cost—let hundreds of people reap the benefit of these plans."

"This is the day of machinery, the day for producing in tremendous quantities, thereby accomplishing in minutes that which would consume hours, days and weeks to achieve by usual methods. After having worked out plans to the highest point of economy, why not cut the materials by labor-saving machines *instead of the old hand method,* thereby reducing labor and waste to a minimum."

> ¶ ALL CHANCES FOR ERRORS AS TO QUANTITY AND QUALITY ARE ELIMINATED BY PURCHASING ALL MATERIALS AT A STATED PRICE FROM ONE COMPANY—FROM BENNETT.

SCIENCE'S ANSWER IS THE BENNETT-WAY

The best designs and plans have been produced for hundreds to share the benefits—a huge modern mill in the heart of the lumber market has been equipped with labor-and-waste-saving machinery of the latest type—and YOU, who want to build a home, reap the advantages and savings of the Bennett-Way in securing one of finer design, greater convenience, and genuine durability.

Perhaps right here, it is well to establish the difference between a Bennett Ready-Cut Home and a portable house.

The object of the portable system is to produce a building construction which may be put together to form a temporary shelter—taken apart again—moved from place to place as desired. Manufacturers of portable buildings cannot and do not represent their products to be permanent.

But Bennett Homes, Better-Built and Ready-Cut, are built for permanency. Once your Bennett Home is completed, there is absolutely no difference between it and any well constructed home, except, perhaps, that our designs are more attractive and impressive than the average homes one sees.

HOW RENT-MONEY COUNTS

This table shows what rent amounts to in ten and twenty years, with six per cent interest compounded annually, and gives an idea of the value of the house one can pay for by applying rent toward paying for a home.

Rent per Month	In 10 Years	In 20 Years
$ 8.00	$1,265.35	$ 3,531.41
12.00	1,898.02	5,279.11
17.00	2,688.86	7,504.24
20.00	3,163.36	8,828.52
25.00	3,954.20	11,035.65
30.00	4,745.04	13,242.78
35.00	5,535.88	15,449.91
50.00	7,908.40	22,071.30

Tonawanda, heart of the Lumber Market. Great lumber-docks on one side, main trunk-line railroads on the other.

ATTRACTIVE DESIGNS

There are more than fifty designs and plans offered on the following pages. They have been carefully and expertly selected from hundreds submitted. These designs are not merely dreams of architects or artists. They are actual houses which have been built, lived in and proven practical and pleasurable in every detail. In considering a BENNETT BETTER-BUILT HOME, you are offered a very wide selection of various styles and sizes, so that you may choose a home that will suit your particular needs, tastes, locality, and pocketbook.

In building the Bennett Way you have this genuine advantage—you know, before you build, just exactly how your home will look after it is completed. Do you know *that* when your local architect or contractor designs your home for you? He may convince you that his design is what you want, and induce you to accept it, even against your own better judgment. Though you may not be pleased with the design he has prepared, nevertheless you accept his ideas rather than submit to the additional expense and delay of a change. BENNETT BETTER-BUILT HOMES correspond in every detail with the actual photographs shown in this catalog. Should the design you select require some slight alterations, we shall be very glad to make such changes, if practical, at actual cost.

ECONOMY IN DRAFTING

The first of a series of savings for you starts in our drafting room.

It is quite necessary for the architect to charge a considerable fee for his drawings, for he must pay expenses and a profit. The drawings for our houses are even more elaborate, and the first cost of production is naturally much greater. Yet there is this gain for you: when the drawings are once made, hundreds of blue prints are made from them at practically a negligible cost. Therefore, we furnish you with blue prints from our drawings *absolutely free* of fees or of any charge.

Two large schooners unloading a giant shipment at the spacious Bennett Docks.

Millions of feet of choice lumber air-drying for your and other fine homes.

ECONOMY IN STANDARDIZATION

Next we help you realize a decided saving through standardization of materials.

In designing an attractive home, a professional architect can give little thought to standard lengths or shapes of material. Our Bennett Better-Built designers, however, put forth both thought and effort toward producing, not only an attractive home, but one which is economical of rough and finished lumber, millwork, etc.

For instance, there are certain standard lengths and widths of lumber, and certain standard styles and sizes of windows, doors, window frames, door frames—in fact of every kind of millwork. Standard items can be manufactured in tremendous quantities at very low cost while special styles and sizes require readjustment of machinery, and the waste (sometimes 33 and 1-3 per cent) of standard-sized materials to meet special requirements. We manufacture such an extensive variety of styles and sizes in building materials of so many kinds, that an appearance as artistic as you may wish can easily be produced without resorting to the expense of special materials.

Another important application of standardization lies in the spacing of windows and the like. Insofar as appearance is concerned, 6 inches one way or another usually makes but little difference in the spacing of windows. But from the standpoint of economy, it is decidedly better to have the spacing in even feet. For instance, windows spaced 12 or 14 feet apart permit the use of 12 or 14 foot standard length boards, without waste; whereas, if the windows were spaced 12′ 6″ apart, it would necessitate the cutting up of a 14′ or 16′ board with a waste on every board that goes to make up the full height of the window.

ECONOMY IN USE OF LABOR-SAVING MACHINERY

By the use of gigantic, powerful machinery, we save you a large percentage of labor cost, and inaccuracies that always waste hand-cut lumber.

The prices quoted in our catalog furnish you with material sufficient to complete every listed detail of the home which you select. In addition, it covers the cost of cutting every

Machines sawing and resawing lumber for homes—saving hours and days over hand methods.

piece of material so that when it reaches its destination, it is ready to nail. There will be no wasting of time waiting for "something forgotten that must be ordered," waiting for one man to cut and fit a part before another can go ahead.

You cannot possible go astray, because—as we said before—our blue prints are thorough and complete, showing the exact location of each and every piece of material. It would not be difficult to erect the entire building with only the blue prints at hand. Nevertheless, to facilitate the work, we furnish a bill of material, itemizing each and every piece, and instructing where it should be placed.

As a further safeguard against error and confusion, we include a set of instructions written by men who have had years of actual experience in constructing houses.

ECONOMY IN CARPENTRY

The entire time consumed by the carpenter for calculating the best plan for framing, has been eliminated. This time is entirely saved, because with our Bennett Better-Built system, the planning is completely done in our office before the material is shipped, and our *Special Notch System* makes the work speedy.

As you have watched work on a house, have you ever stopped to figure how very much of a workman's time was spent in first measuring, then cutting, then trying and perhaps refitting the material—all this as against the very small amount of time required for fastening or nailing? Well, we save you all that fuss and waste by furnishing the material not merely cut, but cut to fit more accurately than hand labor ever could.

Immediately upon receipt of your order, the blue-prints of the design you have selected, the bill of material and a set of instructions are mailed to you. At the same time, a duplicate bill of material is sent into our mill, with instructions to start cutting. Within a few hours the material for

the frame of your house is completed—which means that the work which would have required many days of expensive labor on the job, is accomplished in hours by our machines—more economically, more accurately, many times over.

ECONOMY IN MILLWORK

All Bennett Better-Built doors, windows, door frames, window frames, door trim, window trim and mouldings are manufactured in quantities—therefore at a very low cost of production, of which you derive the benefit. Powerful and precise machines saw and resaw, rout stair stringers, mortise, and fit doors and windows, cut and shape woodwork, smooth and sand all sorts and sizes of lumber—with a quality of fine workmanship in dozen and score lots impossible by any other method.

And remember—any saving in labor must be considered a double saving, because the more time required for the erection of your home, the longer you are paying out money for labor on the new and for rent where you are living.

ECONOMY IN WATER TRANSPORTATION OF RAW MATERIALS

The docks of the Ray H. Bennett Lumber Company, Inc., are located the best of any in North Tonawanda. You will realize the importance to you of location, when we tell you that the largest lumber steamers coming down the great lakes, direct from the saw mills, land at our docks. Thus we are enabled to take advantage of lake-steamer cargo-shipments, and save something for you.

Thousands of doors—absolutely clear grade—knotless, and beautifully grained.

You will also appreciate that we, as buyers of cargoes of lumber totalling millions of feet, are entitled to a lower price than the buyer of a carload of lumber containing only about twenty thousand feet. This impresses the fact that we are in a position to furnish you better quality materials at lower prices. We handle lumber in huge quantities—our stock sizes are secured in big units—therefore, our goods are manufactured and handled at a much lower cost.

You can easily see that our ideal location for the securing of our raw materials means large savings to you. We have enormous stocks on hand at all times and are ideally equipped for fast work.

ECONOMY IN EXCEPTIONAL SHIPPING FACILITIES

North Tonawanda, N. Y., where the Bennett Plant is located, is one of the largest lumber markets in the United States. This is due to the fact that North Tonawanda is a made-to-order center for distribution. Its shipping facilities are conceded to be unsurpassed in the country. Practically all of the great railway systems are in direct connection, enabling us to give you the remarkable service—the vitally important quick shipments—for which we are famed—in which we excel.

ECONOMY IN BENNETT BULK BUYING

We have, as yet, made little mention of our vast purchasing power, nor of the fact that you are purchasing your material at wholesale prices.

We purchase, annually, many millions of feet of material directly from the saw mills, thereby eliminating unnecessary expenses and profits. We buy at rock-bottom prices, less all possible discounts for quantity, for prompt payment, etc.

Window warehouse—thousands of dollars' worth of finely constructed frames ready for glazing.

One of our modern Planers—helping to put the celebrated finish on Bennett interior woodwork.

And then our giant purchases are brought by large lake steamers to our docks and unloaded directly into our yard. On one side our material comes in; it moves almost automatically through our yards to the cutting and finishing mills; it leaves them on the railroad side of our property. With our advantages, the cost of handling is therefore reduced to a minimum which only a few of the largest establishments can hope to equal.

BENNETT ADVANTAGES—In a Nutshell

1. Designs and plans proven the "best" of this country's architectural and practical experts.

2. Elimination of architects' and contractors' fees.

3. Materials from the heart of the lumber market—brand-new, bright stock.

4. Saving of waste through standard sizes, lengths, shapes.

5. Ready-cut, ready-to-erect features as against cut-and-try on the job method.

6. Quantity production of standardized millwork.

7. Transportation and handling charges minimized.

8. Huge buying facilities.

9. Services of an organization, celebrated for its financial strength, for ability and for integrity.

10. All-in-all a real HOME for you and yours at a price that represents the greatest possible value for the money you elect to put into it.

IN every paragraph of these specifications you will note how thoroughly we have planned for strength and endurance in the construction of your home—how we employ only the best grades of lumber, accurately cut and fashioned by the most precise workmanship.

In the first place, please understand the importance of our notched construction. See the photograph in the lower corner of next page. The frames of our houses are a great improvement over the common practice, both in matters of accuracy of fit, of strength and rigidity. The notch method is considered costly when done by hand labor, but it is always considered desirable. The Bennett methods of doing by machines in minutes what would take hours or days by the cut-on-the-job way, gives you extra quality without extra cost.

Another thing we wish you to note is the double and triple strength of joists and studding, where extra stresses are sure to be met, or absolute rigidity is an essential. See the three studs at the corners as shown by the photo of "notch" construction.

Notice that we furnish bridging for floor joists; that our stairs are cut accurately, as in the best houses, instead of using mere nailed-on cleats.

Notice how we select and match interior woods for beauty of grain—how we sand them so they will take a most beautiful finish.

Notice that the outside of our houses—door and window frames, and siding,—is of *Redwood*, celebrated for its extraordinary long life, and so approved by the U. S. Government experts.

Notice our hardware and such items as kitchen cabinets, wardrobes, medicine cabinets, even building paper, and lastly notice our double flooring for both floors.

In every last item, Bennett Homes are truly Better-Built—all in all you will get a most attractive, most livable, most enduring dwelling place, giving you a dollar for dollar value that is unequalled in the lumber market.

General Specifications

DIMENSIONS

All rooms show **actual** inside measurements and not from outside of building to center of inside partition or from center of partition to center of partition, as is sometimes given.

PLANS

One set is furnished with each house. They are so complete in detail, that if carefully followed, it is impossible to go wrong. Reversed plans will be furnished without extra cost.

MATERIALS IN GENERAL

All lumber for Bennett "Better-Built" Homes is shipped directly from enormous stocks in our yards. It is all thoroughly seasoned, and guaranteed equal to or better than the grades specified. Thorough seasoning means less waste and consequently lower freight charges. It also means that shrinkage, bound to occur with green lumber, has occurred before the lumber is cut for your home.

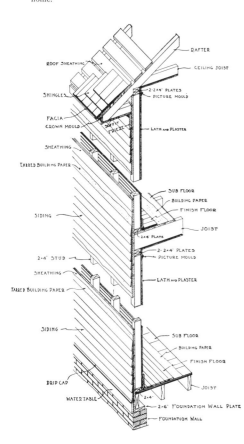

QUANTITY OF MATERIALS

An unqualified guarantee is contained on your order blank that we will furnish material to entirely complete your home in accordance with the following general specifications and with the particular specifications contained on the individual page of photograph and plans.

BASEMENT FRAMES AND SASH

Are not included in your order unless illustration shows siding or shingles to the grade lines, because these are used when the foundation is laid. We plan to have your material on the ground as soon as the foundation is finished and has had sufficient time to set. If we were to furnish basement frames and sash, it would be necessary either to ship them by express, creating additional expense, or it would be necessary to delay the foundation work until the lumber arrived. We cannot see where enough benefit is derived to make up for this additional expense and delay. If, however, you decide to have us furnish them, we will ship them according to your instructions.

FOUNDATION WALL PLATE OR BOND TIMBER

2 in. x 6 in. No. 1 Hemlock, surfaced four sides and cut to fit, furnished to lay on top of the foundation wall to insure an even bearing for the first floor joists.

GIRDER

Size 6 in. x 6 in. or 6 in. x 8 in., (as listed under each design) depending upon the size house. No. 1 Hemlock, surfaced four sides and cut to fit. It is a well-known fact that a built-up timber is stronger than a solid timber, and is much easier to handle. We, therefore, furnish material cut to proper length to make a built-up timber.

GIRDER POSTS

Iron stanchions 4 in. in diameter. These posts are furnished in sufficient number for spacing not more than 8 ft. apart.

FIRST FLOOR JOISTS

2 in. x 8 in. or 2 in. x 10 in. according to span, No. 1 Hemlock, surfaced four sides and cut to fit; spaced 16 in. on centers and **doubled** under all bearing partitions.

SECOND FLOOR JOISTS

2 in. x 8 in. or 2 in. x 10 in. according to span, No. 1 Hemlock, surfaced four sides and cut to fit; spaced 16 in. on centers.

CEILING JOISTS AND COLLAR BEAMS

2 in. x 4 in. or 2 in. x 6 in., depending upon span, No. 1 Hemlock, surfaced four sides and cut to fit; spaced 16 in. on centers.

BRIDGING

2 in. x 2 in. Hemlock, cut to fit. A double row between all 2 in. x 8 in. and 2 in. x 10 in. joists having a span of 12 ft. or over.

RAFTERS

2 in. x 4 in. or 2 in. x 6 in. depending on size of house and pitch of roof, No. 1 Hemlock, surfaced four sides, spaced 24 in. on centers. The rafters are all carefully laid out and cut in our mill, ready to erect on the job.

STUDDING

2 in. x 4 in. No. 1 Hemlock, surfaced four sides, all cut to fit; spaced 16 in. on centers. **Trebled** at corners of outside walls and **doubled** at sides of door and window openings where extra strength is required. Top plates of all partitions and outside walls are **double**; single plates at bottom. Side wall plates are **notched** to receive the studding, a celebrated Bennett feature. It is impossible to set the studding wrong. This is an improvement over the ordinary method of framing. See illustration on opposite page.

WALL SHEATHING

Dressed and matched and cut to fit. This is another important item of Bennett quality. No. 1 Hemlock.

ROOF SHEATHING

1 in. x 4 in. No. 1 Hemlock, surfaced one side, cut to fit. We furnish this material in quantities to allow for 2¼ in. spacing, as is common practice, when shingles are used. In case you decide to use Asphalt Slate Surfaced Roofing, or Asphalt S. S. Shingles, it is necessary to lay the sheathing tightly together. We furnish dressed and matched sheathing for this purpose at a slight additional cost.

PORCH FLOOR JOISTS

2 in. x 6 in. No. 1 Hemlock, surfaced four sides and cut to fit. Spaced 16 in. on centers.

PORCH CEILING JOISTS AND RAFTERS

2 in. x 4 in. No. 1 Hemlock, surfaced four sides and cut to fit. Spaced 24 in. on centers.

SUB FLOORING

1 in. No. 1 Hemlock **Dressed** and **Matched** and cut to fit, furnished for both **first** and **second floors.**

FINISH FLOORING

¹³⁄₁₆ in. x 2¼ in. or ¹³⁄₁₆ in. x 3¼ in. Clear Flat Grain Yellow Pine or Clear Fir. Double Flooring is another proof of the Bennett Better-Built idea—it secures rigidity and soundproofness. Furnished in standard lengths.

PORCH FLOORING

1⅛ in. x 3¼ in. Clear Fir, cut to fit.

PORCH CEILING

⅞ in. Clear Yellow Pine, surfaced and beaded one side and matched, cut to fit.

ATTIC FLOORING

When attic stairs are shown in plans, we furnish $\frac{13}{16}$ in. x $3\frac{1}{4}$ in. No. 2 Yellow Pine, cut to fit. When attic stairs are not shown, no flooring is furnished.

CORNICE CEILING

$\frac{3}{4}$ in. x $3\frac{1}{4}$ in. **Clear Fir,** surfaced and beaded one side and matched, cut to fit, used instead of roof boards over exposed rafter ends.

OUTSIDE FINISH

Clear Redwood, Clear Fir or Sound Knotted White Pine, surfaced four sides.

SIDING

$\frac{1}{2}$ in. **Clear Redwood Bevel Siding, furnished in standard lengths. Or**

Extra *A* Washington Red Cedar Shingles will be furnished instead of siding without extra charge, if so desired. It is commonly known, and an admitted fact that **Redwood is unequalled for exterior protection.**

DOOR FRAMES AND WINDOW FRAMES

Clear Redwood cut to fit, and shipped knocked-down. The sills for all outside doors are $1\frac{3}{4}$ in. x $7\frac{1}{4}$ in. hardwood. All outside casing for window and doors are $\frac{7}{8}$ in. x $4\frac{1}{2}$ in. with drip cap.

INSIDE DOORS

$1\frac{3}{8}$ in. Fir, two or five panel, mortised for lock sets. See pages 36 and 37.

FRONT AND REAR DOORS

Both glazed. Front doors are furnished as shown in the individual house picture. $1\frac{3}{4}$ in. thick No. 1 grade solid Chestnut, unless otherwise specified, **mortised** for front door lock set. Rear door $1\frac{3}{8}$ in., **mortised** for lock set. See pages 36 and 37 for all doors.

ROOF SHINGLES

Extra Clear Washington Red Cedar 5-2 inches, (*) at butt. To lay $4\frac{1}{2}$ in. to the weather. Bennett multi-strip slate-surfaced shingles or Bennett Asphalt Slate-Surfaced Shingles will be furnished at a nominal cost. *Note: The "5 to 2" inches, refers to the thickness of the shingles, and means that five shingles placed one on top of the other with butts together, measures full 2 inches thick at the butt end.

SIDE WALL SHINGLES

For side walls, where shown in catalog, are Premium Brand Extra *A* Washington Red Cedar Shingles 6 to 2, furnished to be laid 5 in. to the weather. Siding will be furnished instead of shingles, if so desired.

SCAFFOLDS AND BRACES

We furnish these as necessary, depending upon the size of the house.

LATH

No. 1 Spruce or Hemlock 48 in. standard. No lath furnished for cellar or attic, unless ordered extra.

GROUNDS

$\frac{5}{8}$ in. x $\frac{7}{8}$ in. Hemlock. To nail around all inside door openings as a guide for plastering.

STAIRS

The stairs are carefully designed for the individual requirements of each home. The material is the highest grade of Yellow Pine to match the beauty of the other interior finish. They are carefully machined in our mills and are shipped to you knocked down, ready to set up. See illustration of manufacture on page 4. See pages 36 and 37 also.

CELLAR AND ATTIC STAIRS

Furnished cut to fit whenever shown in the plans.

PANTRY AND CLOSET SHELVING

Material for shelves is furnished for each closet and pantry, shown in the catalog plans.

KITCHEN CABINET

Whenever kitchen cabinets are shown in the plans they are included in the price for the home. They are shipped to you in the knock-down complete (including hardware). The material is clear grade Yellow Pine See pages 36 and 37.

MEDICINE CABINET

A built-in medicine cabinet is furnished with each house having a bathroom. Each cabinet is complete in every detail and includes a bevel-mirror door. Shipped ready to set in place. See pages 36 and 37.

COLONNADES

Where a colonnade is shown in the plans, it is included in the price of the home. The material is, of course, Yellow Pine to match the other fine interior finish of the home. Each colonnade is manufactured in own own mill under our own supervision, and we guarantee you the very best of materials and the finest workmanship. Two styles of colonnades are shown on pages 36 and 37 of our catalog. In case a colonnade is not included in the plan of the house you select, and you wish to install one, we will, upon application, gladly quote prices.

INSIDE DOOR AND WINDOW TRIM

Clear Yellow Pine of the finest quality obtainable, all carefully matched and sanded. The casings are $1\frac{1}{8}$ in. x $3\frac{5}{8}$ in. in width; back band $1\frac{1}{8}$ in. x $1\frac{1}{8}$ in.; the window stool $\frac{7}{8}$ in. x $3\frac{5}{8}$ in.; the apron $\frac{7}{8}$ in. x $3\frac{1}{4}$ in. This design is one of the choicest on the market. See pages 36 and 37.

BASE, PICTURE MOULDING, CHAIR RAIL AND HOOK STRIPS

Clear Yellow Pine, shipped in standard lengths to be cut on the job; base $\frac{13}{16}$ in. x $7\frac{5}{8}$ in. on first floor. $\frac{13}{16}$ in. x $5\frac{5}{8}$ in. for second floor. Picture moulding $\frac{13}{16}$ in. x $1\frac{1}{2}$ in. Chair rail $\frac{5}{8}$ in. x $3\frac{1}{2}$ in. Hook strips $\frac{13}{16}$ in. x $2\frac{3}{4}$ in. Chair rail for kitchen and bath. Hook strips for all closets.

WINDOWS

$1\frac{3}{8}$ in. Clear White Pine. check rail, made to be used with pulleys and weights. Glass set in and puttied. Styles to correspond with those shown in the individual house pictures. All windows more than 26 inches in width, glazed with **double** strength glass.

PORCH MATERIAL

All porch materials are manufactured from the best weather-resisting woods of standard designs. Porch steps are painstakingly cut to fit in our mill and shipped to you knocked-down with $1\frac{1}{8}$ in. treads.

HARDWARE

MORTISE LOCK SETS

Design illustrated on pages 36 and 37. Furnished in two styles of finish—Antique Copper, or Sand Blast Dull Brass. Unless otherwise specified in your order, we will furnish the Antique Copper. A cylinder front door lock set is furnished with all houses listed at $2400.00 or more. For houses listed at less, the standard bit key front door lock set is furnished.

DOUBLE ACTING FLOOR HINGES AND DOOR PLATES

Furnished with all houses shown with a double swinging door between the kitchen and dining room.

HINGES

Finished to match other hardware. Three hinges are furnished on all front doors.

SASH LIFT, SASH LOCKS AND WINDOW STOP ADJUSTERS

Furnished for all sliding sash windows, finished to match the lock sets, two sash lifts to each window.

BATHROOM HARDWARE

All bathroom hardware is **nickel plated.**

KITCHEN CUPBOARD AND CABINET HARDWARE

All **hinges, turns, etc.,** are included in price quoted and furnished to match other hardware.

NAILS

Sufficient quantities of all sizes furnished for all purposes. Galvanized nails for shingles.

BUILDING PAPER

Tarred Paper is furnished for underneath the siding, and between the finish and sub-flooring.

DOORBELL

We furnish an attractive front door bell set.

MISCELLANEOUS HARDWARE

Our hardware list includes sash cord, window weights, attic sash sets, base knobs, coat hooks, chimney flashing and valley tin, but does not include eavetroughing.

PAINTS, OILS AND VARNISHES

EXTRA FINE QUALITY READY-MIXED PAINT

Sufficient in quantity for three good coats on outside walls. A special hard drying floor paint is furnished to cover the porch floor and steps two coats. Color card furnished upon request.

SPAR VARNISH

Although it costs less to furnish paint for the porch ceiling, we are furnishing a high grade spar varnish for two coats. Spar varnish is also furnished to cover the front door.

INTERIOR VARNISH

A very high grade varnish is furnished for two good coats on all doors, windows and interior trim. This varnish is exceedingly durable and can be rubbed within 36 to 48 hours. It is not affected by hot or cold water and will not crack.

Practically every home owner prefers his bathroom painted rather than varnished. All bathrooms in Bennett Better-Built Homes are especially attractive, owing to the fact that they are finished in white enamel and all hardware is furnished nickel plated. Enamel undercoater is furnished to cover the woodwork, two coats. Two coats of Bennett White Enamel on top of this makes an attractive and durable surface. Our White Enamel Paint will not turn yellow. Putty, oil, sandpaper and turpentine in proper quantities to meet requirements are furnished.

Although we do not include floor varnish or wall paints in our specifications, owing to the wide variety of ways for finishing floors and walls, we will upon request be glad to figure your exact needs and quote upon them.

SHINGLE STAIN

When shingles are used on outside walls, we furnish shingle stain instead of paint. We do not furnish stain for roof shingles, except at an additional cost or order.

FOUNDATION, CHIMNEY, FIREPLACES

Although we show on our plans, the location of foundation, chimney, fireplace, etc., we do not include these items in our prices, nor do we carry the materials in stock. The express and freight charges to be met in shipment would offset any advantages we might offer. For the same reason, we do not furnish plaster. We will, however, gladly co-operate with our customers by offering suggestions or furnishing data regarding same.

PLUMBING, HEATING AND LIGHTING

See pages 71 and 72 for plumbing, heating and lighting fixtures.

The quotations covering the installation of plumbing, heating and lighting equipment vary so much that it is advisable to consider each separately.

Our Equipment Department will furnish you with information and estimates.

Notches Make Assembling Easy

Avon

**26 ft. x 40 ft.
over all
7 Rooms and
Bath**

What "Sterling" means to silver, our "Avon" means to the semi-bungalow home. It is the hallmark of genuine worth.

Rarely do you find so stately, yet so graceful lines. Consider the broad and downward sweeping roofs of main structure and porch, the overhanging eaves, the supporting brackets, the solid pillars and house-wide veranda. And such a wonderful place inside! You'll hesitate a minute in the vestibule—but it's in the hospitable living room you wish to be. There's a restful hearth and fireside at the farther end; or, if you prefer, a triple window to give a wide view of outdoors. And—what's unique—the stairway rising charmingly from one corner of the roomy, cheerful dining room. The kitchen is compact, convenient.

And think of it—*two* airy, sizable bedrooms on the main floor. Yet there are two more sleeping rooms —one extra large—the bath, storeroom, and a linen closet upstairs. Notice the ample closet room, the coat closet, the flood of light and air possible in every room of this home.

Oh! there are features in the "Avon" to tell you about for a long time—but write us you are interested in it especially, and we will send the whole splendid story.

SPECIFICATIONS

Ceiling height first floor approximately 9 ft.
Ceiling height second floor approximately 8 ft.
Girders 6 in. x 8 in.
First and second floor joists 2 in. x 8 in.
Ceiling joists 2 in. x 4 in.   Rafters 2 in. x 6 in.
Front door—our "Chautauqua," of solid Chestnut, 3 ft. x 6 ft. 8 in. and 1¾ in. thick, glazed with clear glass. *See pages 36–37.*
French doors between vestibule and living room. *See pages 36–37.*
Prices on oak floors and trim for vestibule, living room and dining room, maple flooring in kitchen, quoted on application.
Our No. 1 kitchen cupboard and medicine cabinet included in the selling price. *See pages 36–37.*

See pages 8–9 for general specifications.

KITCHEN
14·0·12·3

BED ROOM
10·6·11·0

CLO   CLO

DINING ROOM
14·0·12·6

BED ROOM
10·6·11·0

COATS.

LIVING ROOM
17·3·13·3

VESTIBULE
7·3·9·9

PORCH
26·10

· AVON ·

FIRST FLOOR PLAN·

BATH
7·2·8·11

BED ROOM
9·10·12·9

LIN CLO

CLOSET

HALL

CLO

STORE ROOM
11·9·7·6

BED ROOM
15·6·15·3

ROOF

· AVON ·

SECOND FLOOR PLAN

Charlotte

26 ft. x 38 ft. over all
8 Rooms, Vestibule, Bath

There's a quiet, rich dignity to the Charlotte—a home beyond the ordinary for a good-sized family. The shingle sides are novel and pleasing. Interesting brackets support the wide, overhanging eaves. Dormers provide triple windows—one, a bay!

You enter a cozy reception hall, with its pretty stairway and landing. An attractive colonnade arch leads into a well lighted living room. Here you may have your cozy fireplace—or, if you prefer, none at all. French doors communicate with an unusually attractive dining room. Many will be pleased with the bedroom and bath on first floor. Note the splendid bedrooms with roomy closets on second floor—bath with an easy access, a linen closet, a large kitchen cabinet.

Truly, the Charlotte is an *achievement*—in rare design—in perfection of every detail—in wonderful value for its low price.

SPECIFICATIONS

Ceiling height first floor approximately 9 ft.

Ceiling height second floor approximately 8 ft.

Girders 6 in. x 8 in.

First and second floor joists 2 in. x 8 in.

Ceiling joists 2 in. x 4 in.   Rafters 2 in. x 6 in.

Front door—our "Conesus," of solid Chestnut, 3 ft. x 6 ft. 8 in. and 1¾ in. thick. *See pages 36–37.*

French doors between living room and dining room.

Niagara Colonnade between hall and living room. *See pages 36–37.*

Prices on oak floors and trim for vestibule, living room and dining room, maple flooring in kitchen, quoted on application.

Our No. 1 kitchen cupboard and two medicine cabinets included in selling price. *See pages 36–37.*

See pages 8–9 for general specifications.

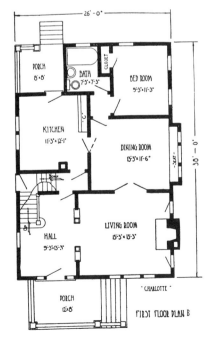

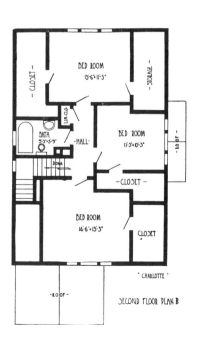

Bryant

28 ft. x 24 ft. over all
6 Rooms and Bath

If your desires lean toward the home beautiful, yet modest, containing all necessary conveniences for modern living, you will study the Bryant with considerable interest.

Though of complete styling, it is unburdened with expensive "fuss and feathers." The roof treatment is artistically handled on porch, dormer and sides. A shingled second story adds to the smart effect.

A good-sized porch leads to a spacious living room, while to the right stands a gem of a dining room. Especially mark the stairway, closed or open as you may wish—and a distinct gain in conservation of warmth in cold weather. Off the nearby kitchen is a dandy storage closet. The downstairs bedroom may be as readily used for den or study.

Upstairs there is a convenient bathroom, and two roomy sleeping chambers with extra large closets. There is the innovation of a bright sewing room—a room all for mother.

Splendidly designed, sturdily built in every detail, you can choose the Bryant as a home that will meet your future as well as present needs.

SPECIFICATIONS

Ceiling height first floor approximately 9 ft.
Ceiling height second floor approximately 8 ft.
Girders 6 in. x 8 in.
First and second floor joists 2 in. x 8 in.
Ceiling joists 2 in. x 4 in. Rafters 2 in. x 6 in.
Front door—our "Mohawk," of solid Chestnut, 3 ft. x 6 ft. 8 in. and 1¾ in. thick, glazed with clear glass. *See pages 36–37.*
Our No. 2 kitchen cupboard and medicine cabinet included in the selling price. *See pages 36–37.*

See pages 8–9 for general specifications.

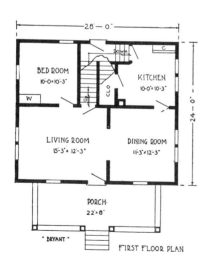

FIRST FLOOR PLAN

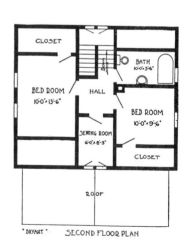

SECOND FLOOR PLAN

Batavia, N. Y.
Nov. 11, 1917.

Gentlemen:—

Five years ago I bought all my lumber from you to build my house and I am very much pleased with it. I saved a good big bit by dealing with you.

R. P.

Ilion

**22 ft. x 34 ft.
over all
8 Rooms,
Bath, Pantry**

Trimness is personified by this neat, compact, all-shingle house—trimness and comfort, for the common-sense interior arrangement is in keeping with the all-around beauty and durability of the exterior.

Notice that you reach the porch by means of the steps on the side—this advantage securing fine privacy for time spent on the veranda.

One enters a reception hall that opens either toward the amply-spaced living room, or a quiet den (which might readily be used as an office, if desired). The dining room is complete with a triple-window bay, insuring a wealth of light and an ideal place for house-plants and flowers. The kitchen and the generous pantry are in that close proximity which modern home management dictates nowadays. Side and rear doors are combined in an entrance at grade.

And then step upstairs! Three bright, airy, double-windowed bedrooms greet you—rooms of liberal width and depth, each one having an adjoining extra-size closet.

Taken altogether, the Ilion is a home every foot useful—spacious yet compact —best of all, quite reasonable.

SPECIFICATIONS

Ceiling height first floor approximately 9 ft.

Ceiling height second floor approximately 8 ft.

Girders 6 in. x 8 in.

First and second floor joists 2 in. x 8 in.

Ceiling joists and rafters 2 in. x 4 in.

Front door—our "Saranac," of Solid Chestnut, 3 ft. x 6 ft. 8 in. and 1¾ in. thick, glazed with clear glass. *See pages 36–37.*

Cased opening between reception hall and living room and between living room and dining room.

Windows divided upper sash as shown in illustration.

See pages 8–9 for general specifications.

FIRST FLOOR PLAN

SECOND FLOOR PLAN

Harvard

**22 ft. x 24 ft. over all
6 Rooms and Bath**

The Harvard possesses a style and character peculiarly its own. Distinctly modern in arrangement and construction—both the exterior and interior arrangement showing thought and care. The broken roof lines, hooded entrance and pergola porch are the attractive exterior features. The living room is large and cheerful, well lighted from all sides. An attractive stair leads from this room to the second floor.

The dining room is very attractive with grouped windows at the side and a French door opening onto the private porch. The kitchen is of a convenient size and well lighted. Our cupboard No. 2 illustrated on page 37 is a part of the finish in this room and is supplied as a part of the equipment. Direct access from kitchen to front door is had without passing through other rooms.

Space for refrigerator, etc., is provided in cellar entryway. The cellar stairway arrangement is very convenient from both kitchen and front part of house, provides a side entrance and does away with extra expense of outside cellar stairs.

The second floor is divided into three comfortable bedrooms and a bath, the latter being easily accessible to all rooms and stairs. Large wardrobes are provided for two of the bedrooms and off the front bedroom is a large closet for storage.

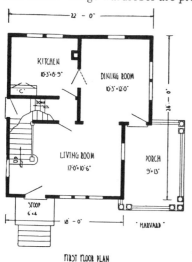

FIRST FLOOR PLAN

SPECIFICATIONS

Ceiling height first floor approximately 9 ft.

Ceiling height second floor approximately 8 ft.

Girders 6 in. x 8 in.

First and second floor joists 2 in. x 8 in.

Ceiling joists and rafters 2 in. x 4 in.

Front door—our "Mohawk" of solid Chestnut, 3 ft. x 6 ft. 8 in. and 1¾ in. thick, glazed with clear glass. *See pages 36-37.*

Our kitchen cupboard No. 2, wardrobe and medicine cabinet included in the selling price. *See pages 36-37.*

See pages 8-9 for general specifications.

Raymond

24 ft. x 24 ft. over all
6 Rooms and Bath

Good taste is exemplified in every line of the Raymond. It has been well described as "most prosperous looking." The consistent use of wide clapboarding is indeed a pleasing feature, and there is a touch of genuine originality in the roof treatment around the front dormer. The roominess of the wide veranda is a harmonizing part of the generous proportions of the whole.

A luxurious living room greets you as you enter from the vestibule. The dining room, just to the rear and on a corner gladdens you with its brightness. Your attention is also called to the plentiful light provided throughout—six windows in the living room, three in the dining room and three in the kitchen.

The same cheerfulness is continued in the arrangement of the three spacious bedrooms upstairs. Each sleeping room has its own closet or wardrobe, and the bathroom is conveniently placed near the head of the stairs.

It seems hardly true that such substantiality in the design, such desirability in the arrangement, could be secured in dimensions 24 ft. x 24 ft. But the Raymond proves how beautiful, practical, substantial, Bennett Homes are.

SPECIFICATIONS

Ceiling height first floor approximately 9 ft.
Ceiling height second floor approximately 8 ft.
Girders 6 in. x 8 in.
First and second floor joists 2 in. x 8 in.
Ceiling joists 2 in. x 4 in.   Rafters 2 in. x 6 in.
Front door—our "Mohawk," of solid Chestnut, 3 ft. x 6 ft. 8 in. and 1¾ in. thick, glazed with clear glass. *See pages 36–37.*
Our No. 1 kitchen cupboard and medicine cabinet included in the selling price. *See pages 36–37.*

See pages 8–9 for general specifications.

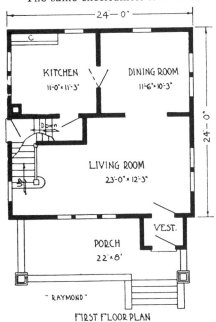

" RAYMOND "

FIRST FLOOR PLAN

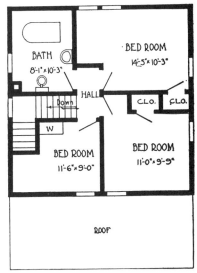

" RAYMOND "

SECOND FLOOR PLAN

15

Lincoln

30 ft. x 26 ft. over all
7 Rooms and Bath

Some of the most artistic homes are those provided with a slightly terraced lawn, porch and first floor practically at grade. The Lincoln is a strikingly attractive example of such a plan. Seemingly a part of the landscape on which it rests, it blends itself easily into all its surroundings.

As you step onto the veranda, you are struck by its wide expanse—while before you an attractive door with little side windows holds your admiration. A hospitable fireplace commands your attention as you enter, and you marvel at the brightness of the whole room, for there are in reality two sides practically of glass. A very large opening calls your attention to a dining room made most tempting by a window seat just under triple windows. If you wish to retire for a quiet conversation, a bit of rest or reading, the cozy den satisfies your every wish.

The stairway to the second floor is hidden, but ascends easily to a large halfway landing, and then reverses to the second story. Here you find two splendid bedrooms, each with ample closet space, and a slightly smaller room, balancing the bathroom on the other corner!—conveniently near which is a linen closet.

Notice especially in the front bedrooms the casement windows opening underneath the dormer roof. Notice, too, that in one of these bedrooms you might easily have your upstairs fireplace.

For the average family with tastes that run to homes with personality, we sincerely believe the Lincoln offers a real first choice.

SPECIFICATIONS

Ceiling height first floor approximately 9 ft.
Ceiling height second floor approximately 8 ft.
Girders 6 in. x 8 in.
First and second floor joists 2 in. x 8 in.
Ceiling joists 2 in. x 4 in. Rafters 2 in. x 6 in.
Front door—special design of solid Chestnut, 3 ft. x 6 ft. 8 in., 1¾ in. thick, glazed with clear glass.
Prices on oak floors and trim for vestibule, living room and dining room, maple flooring in kitchen, quoted on application.
Our kitchen cupboard No. 1 and medicine cabinet included in the selling price. *See pages 36–37.*

See pages 8–9 for general specifications.

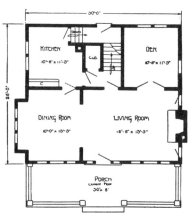

FIRST FLOOR PLAN

SECOND FLOOR PLAN

Franklin

**24 ft. x 32 ft. over all
7 Rooms and Bath**

For such modest proportions there are few homes presenting greater roominess than the Franklin. Think of it—only 32 ft. long and 24 ft. wide, yet containing a 23 ft. living room, a sizable dining room and kitchen, three comfortable bedrooms, and an additional sewing room, and nursery or extra bedroom.

The generous veranda of this house is a distinctive feature. Notice the graceful harmony between slope of the porch and the main roof. See the brackets, and the exposed rafters. Consider the well-chosen position of the dormers, left and right, the latter being the only one in view from where you look.

Out of the living room mounts a pretty stairway. At the right, a wide opening leads to a delightful dining room. The kitchen connects with a double swinging door, and besides the cabinet contains a closet with room enough to serve a number of purposes. There's a bedroom on the first floor, with its own large closet.

Upstairs—two good-sized bedrooms, both with large closets, and an extra room all centering on the upstairs hall. Notice that a complete bath is here. Particularly note that there are two windows in each bedroom.

It's no wonder that the Franklin is a popular choice among Bennett owners. Such roominess, such completeness is rarely found in a home so inexpensive.

SPECIFICATIONS

Ceiling height first floor approximately 9 ft.
Ceiling height second floor approximately 8 ft.
Girders 6 in. x 8 in.
First and second floor joists 2 in. x 8 in.
Ceiling joists 2 in. x 4 in. Rafters 2 in. x 6 in.
Front door—our "Mohawk," of solid Chestnut, 3 ft. x 6 ft. 8 in. and 1¾ in. thick, glazed with clear glass.
Our kitchen cupboard No. 1 and two medicine cabinets included in the selling price. *See pages 36–37.*

See pages 8–9 for general specifications.

FIRST FLOOR PLAN B

SECOND FLOOR PLAN B

Potomac

26 ft. x 38 ft. over all
8 Rooms and Bath

Summer or winter, indoors or out, the Potomac is a place of happiness, contentment and comfort for any family.

It would seem that our architects have outdone themselves on the exterior of this home. The overhanging second story, spacious porch and solid chimney, pattern of shingling—these features and a score of others speak for themselves.

But perhaps it is on the interior that **our** designers have secured the most remarkable results. The front door opens on a beautiful living room extending the house width, stairs at the left leading to a halfway landing. Nearby perhaps you may locate your broad fireplace and hearth. Graceful French doors yield from this living room upon a sunny dining room—that, in turn, opens upon a first-floor bedroom, and, through a double swinging door, the nicely ordered kitchen.

Note well that adjoining four-windowed breakfast room. Picture the youngsters and yourselves seated at its sun-flooded table upon its built-in seats, starting the day right in its cozy, cheery atmosphere.

Underneath the broad sloping roof are three most attractive bedrooms. There are two large closets and a wardrobe, and the bath is easily reached from any sleeping room.

The Potomac is indeed a home you will like living in—beauty, utility, endurance to delight you for years to come.

SPECIFICATIONS

Ceiling height first floor approximately 9 ft.
Ceiling height second floor approximately 8 ft.
Girders 6 in. x 8 in.
First and second floor joists 2 in. x 8 in.
Ceiling joists 2 in. x 4 in. Rafters 2 in. x 6 in.
Front door—our "Mohawk," of solid Chestnut, 3 ft. x 6 ft. 8 in. and 1¾ in. thick, glazed with clear glass. *See pages 36–37.*
Breakfast table and seats included in selling price.
Our No. 2 kitchen cupboard and medicine cabinet included in the selling price. *See pages 36–37.* Awning not included.

See pages 8–9 for general specifications.

FIRST FLOOR PLAN

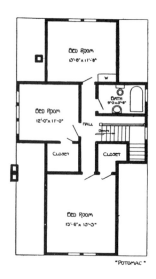

SECOND FLOOR PLAN

New Hartford

26 ft. x 24 ft. over all
6 Rooms and Bath

Distinction has been remarkably well attained in this little gem of a home. The clever treatment of the front—novel porch pillars, lattice work and white trim—makes a neat and artistic contrast with the darker tones of the shingled body of the house.

The porch is one of those all-embracing verandas, broad enough for the whole family and their friends. Living and dining room are each amply proportioned, with wide opening between, making large space available for dances, parties, and such affairs. The downstairs bedroom might just as well be a den, study or private office, if preferred.

The second floor sleeping quarters are well lighted, with the opportunity for cozy window corners under the dormer. Placing an enclosed stairway at the rear of the house is a fortunate departure in a home of this size, from the accustomed practice—just one more example of the all-around distinctiveness of this appealing home.

One man who has built many homes and sold them, runs to the New Hartford as his "best bet". You, too, will find this distinctive home a most livable—or if you prefer, a most salable place.

FIRST FLOOR PLAN

SPECIFICATIONS

Ceiling height first floor approximately 9 ft.

Ceiling height second floor approximately 8 ft.

Girders 6 in. x 8 in.

First and second floor joists 2 in. x 8 in.

Ceiling joists 2 in. x 4 in.

Rafters 2 in. x 6 in.

Front door—our "Mohawk," of solid Chestnut, 3 ft. x 6 ft. 8 in., 1¾ in. thick, glazed with clear glass. *See pages 36–37.*

Cased opening between living room and dining room.

Our No. 1 kitchen cupboard and medicine cabinet included in the selling price.

See pages 8–9 for general specifications.

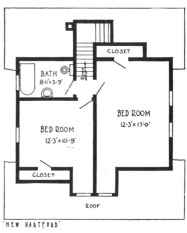

SECOND FLOOR PLAN

Niagara

24 ft. x 30 ft. over all
6 Rooms, Bath, Hall

Here's a home of comfort and contentment in the highest degree. Rich simplicity marks every item of its ingenious architecture—and its pleasing and practical arrangement means a most satisfying livableness for a modest sized family.

There are crisp, clean-cut lines from the tip of its gable down to its very foundations. The shingled triangles in green, the gently sloping roofs, the generous porch and its pillars, the details of the trim—all add their bit to the striking appearance of the whole.

But let's call and see the interior. Here's a charming reception hall for a first glimpse. A broad archway points the way to a sociable living room, amply provided with windows yet with plenty of space for piano and furniture. A splendid dining room, with outlook to the side and rear, connects to a compact but uncrowded kitchen.

Ascending the rich stairway by two easy flights, we come upon a cheerful front bedroom—with a closet to enthuse the most exacting wife. Just a step back is the complete bath—and nearby are the other sleeping chambers, again each with spacious closet room.

But now, we rest our case with you. One last word—if the Niagara *satisfies* your needs and pocketbook, we sincerely assure you that enduring happiness and comfort will be your reward in it.

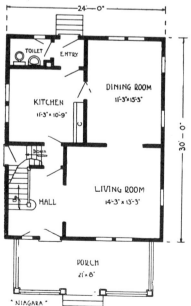

SPECIFICATIONS

Ceiling height first floor approximately 9 ft.
Ceiling height second floor approximately 8 ft.
Girders 6 in. x 8 in.
First and second floor joists 2 in. x 8 in.
Ceiling joists 2 in. x 4 in. Rafters 2 in. x 4 in.
Front door—our "Chautauqua," of solid Chestnut,
    3 ft. x 6 ft. 8 in. and 1¾ in. thick, glazed
    with clear glass. *See pages 36–37.*
Prices on oak floors and trim in hall, living room
    and dining room, maple flooring in kitchen,
    quoted on application.
Our No. 1 kitchen cupboard and medicine cabinet
    included in the selling price. *See pages 36–37.*

See pages 8–9 for general specifications.

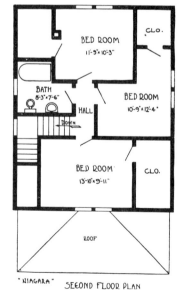

LaSalle

26 ft. x 36 ft. over all
8 Rooms, 2 Baths

Inviting—Distinctive—Practical! This description reveals the secret of the LaSalle's great popularity. Note the artistic overhanging eaves—and the dormers, in front and on either side. These give balance and substantiality. They afford, too, the roominess of a one and one-half story home, with the smart lines of a semi-bungalow design.

See how well-lighted are the bedrooms. Particularly note the ample closet room. And one room upstairs might well be used as a den, sewing room, or nursery.

There is a cosy, sunny bay window in the dining room—there is a window seat there! The roomy, well-protected porch is a splendid feature. The kitchen is ample, but most compact and convenient. And the two bathrooms, one on each floor, give a final touch to an ideal plan.

SPECIFICATIONS

Ceiling height first floor approximately 9 ft.
Ceiling height second floor approximately 8 ft.
Girders 6 in. x 8 in.
First and second floor joists 2 in. x 8 in.
Ceiling joists 2 in. x 4 in.
Rafters 2 in. x 6 in.
Front door—our "Chautauqua," of solid Chestnut, 3 ft. x 6 ft. 8 in. and 1¾ in. thick, glazed with clear glass. *See pages 36–37.*
Prices on oak floors and trim for living room and dining room, maple flooring in kitchen, quoted on application.
Our No. 1 kitchen cupboard and two medicine cabinets included in the selling price. *See pages 36–37.*

See pages 8–9 for general specifications.

FIRST FLOOR PLAN LA SALLE

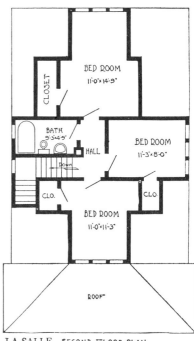

LA SALLE SECOND FLOOR PLAN

21

Bison

**24 ft. x 24 ft.
over all
5 Rooms
and Bath**

For the family interested in a permanent abode that shall combine utility with refined architectural features, the Bison is a home with a genuine appeal.

Every line of its design bespeaks good taste. Especially unique is its undercut porch, a place wide and roomy for the whole family and guests, too. The unusual treatment of railing, brickwork and pillars also makes it distinctly attractive.

The living room always proves a great attraction—both to the family and to visitors. A handsome stairway leads upward from the left of this bright room, while the inviting dining room with its prized bay window greets you through a pretty colonnade. The kitchen is compact, light, and equipped with a labor-saving cabinet.

Upstairs, also, you will find the same combination of bright, cheerful quarters. The bathroom is nearby, and large closet and storage room serve for keeping some family belongings without cluttering up the useful rooms.

Surely the Bison would make you a most livable home!

SPECIFICATIONS

Ceiling height first floor approximately 9 ft.

Ceiling height second floor approximately 8 ft.

Girders 6 in. x 8 in.

First and second floor joists 2 in. x 8 in.

Ceiling joists 2 in. x 4 in.   Rafters 2 in. x 6 in.

Front door—our "Conesus," of solid Chestnut, 3 ft. x 6 ft. 8 in. and 1¾ in. thick, glazed with clear glass.

Colonnade arch between living room and dining room. *See pages 36–37.*

Our No. 1 kitchen cupboard and medicine cabinet included in the selling price. *See pages 36–37.*

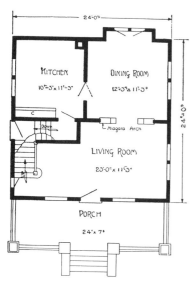

FIRST FLOOR PLAN

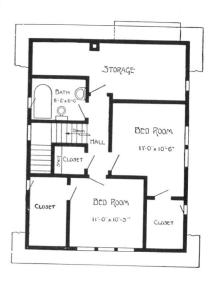

SECOND FLOOR PLAN

See pages 8–9 for general specifications.

Ideal
26 ft. x 28 ft. over all
6 Rooms, Bath, Alcove

The Ideal might well be termed "A big little home." Attractiveness here is gained by clever application of symmetry and proportion. The broad porch with unique columns could easily be converted into an outdoor living room with screens in summer and glass in winter.

The interior is cheerful and homelike. The living room and dining room, connected by a wide cased opening, may be used as one on occasions. A grade entrance is included in the rear, so that the basement may be reached from outdoors without passing through the kitchen. Note, too, the refrigerator may be iced from outdoors.

At the head of the stairs on the second floor is the bath, in an "ideal" location, convenient to all bedrooms, also economically located for plumbing. The alcove provides a sewing room or a child's bedroom.

SPECIFICATIONS

Ceiling height first floor approximately 9 ft.

Ceiling height second floor approximately 8 ft.

First and second floor joists 2 in. x 8 in.

Ceiling joists 2 in. x 4 in. Rafters 2 in. x 6 in.

Front door—our "Saranac," of solid Chestnut, 3 ft. x 6 ft. 8 in. and 1¾ in. thick, glazed with clear glass. *See pages 36–37.*

Prices on oak floors and trim for living room and dining room, maple flooring in kitchen, quoted on application.

Our No. 1—6 ft. pantry cabinet in pantry. *See pages 36–37.*

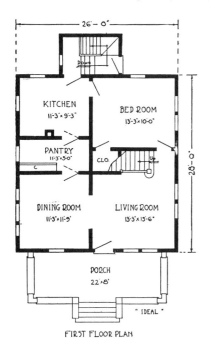

FIRST FLOOR PLAN

SECOND FLOOR PLAN

See pages 8–9 for general specifications.

Hamilton

**28 ft. x 36 ft. over all
8 Rooms and Bath**

Examine the Hamilton minutely and you will agree that it embodies most, if not all, of the attributes of that "Dream Home" which you have so long planned.

While it doesn't lack a single detail of that refined architecture which our modern standards demand, it nevertheless is a most practical dwelling-place.

Note the dignified yet tasteful exterior design—the good-looking foundation, spacious porch, and graceful dormers on front and sides. Then look within—a generous living room with cheery fireplace, liberal-sized dining room, a secluded retreat in the form of the den, convenient kitchen, and three large, light, airy bedrooms and bath upstairs.

In the Hamilton you have all advantages of the semi-bungalow construction—compactness and proper economy—combined with the ample elbow-room of a full-sized home, designed and built for lifetime usage—and sufficiently reasonable to be within the means of most folks with home-owning aspirations.

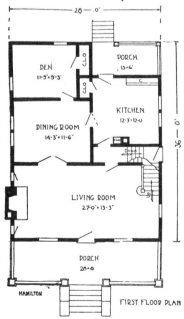

SPECIFICATIONS

Ceiling height first floor approximately 9 ft.

Ceiling height second floor approximately 8 ft.

Girders 6 in. x 8 in.

First and second floor joists 2 in. x 8 in.

Ceiling joists 2 in. x 4 in. Rafters 2 in. x 6 in.

Front door—our "Chautauqua," of solid Chestnut, 3 ft. x 6 ft. 8 in. and 1¾ in. thick, glazed with clear glass. *See pages 36–37.*

French doors between living room and dining room. *See pages 36–37.*

Prices on oak floors and trim for living room and dining room, maple flooring in kitchen, quoted on application.

Our No. 1 kitchen cupboard and medicine cabinet included in selling price. *See pages 36–37.*

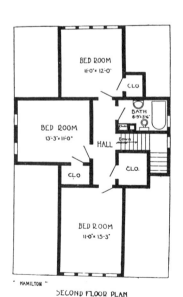

See pages 8–9 for general specifications.

Fulton

28 ft. x 26 ft. over all
7 Rooms and Bath

The Fulton is true to its type—a very happy appearance combined with a very desirable plan. The broad, sloping roof, broken by a well-formed dormer, and unusually wide porch lend dignity to the whole exterior of this home. If one wishes, shingles may well be used in the place of the siding protecting the first story, and variegated colors used in soft-toned effects.

You enter the Fulton through the charming reception hall. From there the stairway winds to the second story. There's a wide cased opening introducing you to the living room, at one end of which you may have an inviting fireplace built if you wish. The dining room receives light from two sides. Between it and kitchen is a pantry, both exits enclosed by double-swinging doors.

The upstairs of this home consists of three fine sleeping rooms, each with an extra large closet. The plan is finally completed by the usual bath.

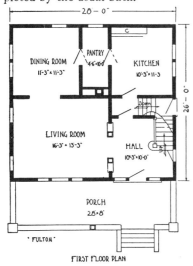

FIRST FLOOR PLAN

In a setting of trees and bushes, this home is truly pleasing, and combined with its most livable plan and low price, offers the soundest kind of an investment for the home builder.

SPECIFICATIONS

Ceiling height first floor approximately 9 ft.
Ceiling height second floor approximately 8 ft.
Girders 6 in. x 8 in.
First and second floor joists 2 in. x 8 in.
Ceiling joists 2 in. x 4 in. Rafters 2 in. x 6 in.
Front door—special design, of solid Chestnut, 3 ft. x 6 ft. 8 in. and 1¾ in. thick, glazed with clear glass.
Niagara colonnade between hall and living room.
Our kitchen cupboard No. 1 and medicine cabinet included in the selling price.

See pages 8-9 for general specifications.

SECOND FLOOR PLAN

Cleo

28 ft. x 36 ft. over all
6 Rooms, 1 Bath

Here is an unsurpassed bungalow—in architecture, in arrangement, in convenience.

Wide eaves, exposed rafter ends, perfect harmony of line, a substantial porch that excels in charm —these delight from without.

And within!—An ideal floor plan affords three well-lighted bedrooms, a spacious living room, well-arranged kitchen and bath conveniently located to all rooms, and made desirably private by a small hall. Between living and dining rooms is an impressive colonnade arch. There's the luxury of a fireplace if you wish it—and high casement windows at either side with nooks beneath for bookcases or furniture.

Saugerties, N. Y. Mar 2 1920

M Ray N Bennett Lumber Co

To GEO. T. BARTELS, Mr.

CARPENTER AND BUILDER

Dear sir received the material i bought from you for my house i find it much better than i though it would be it is the best i ever had from iny firm yet our dealer says it cant be as good as his for the money i will show it to him some day and then he can be his own Judge i will do all i can for you to gain more customers thank you for the promptness and square deal given me i remain yours Truly

Geo T Bartels
26 Allen St
Saugerties N Y
please send me one of your mill books & hard ware books

Truly unusual is the Cleo!—truly beautiful, truly roomy, truly practical, and best of all, modestly priced.

SPECIFICATIONS

Ceiling height first floor approximately 9 ft.

Girders 6 in. x 8 in.

First floor joists 2 in. x 8 in.   Rafters 2 in. x 6 in.

Ceiling joists 2 in. x 4 in.

Front door—our "Mohawk," of solid Chestnut, 3 ft. x 6 ft. 8 in. and 1¾ in. thick, glazed with clear glass. *See pages 36–37.*

Prices on oak floors and trim for living room and dining room, maple flooring in kitchen, quoted on application.

Wardrobe in rear bedroom.

Our kitchen cupboard No. 2 and medicine cabinet included in the selling price. *See pages 36–37.*

See pages 8–9 for general specifications.

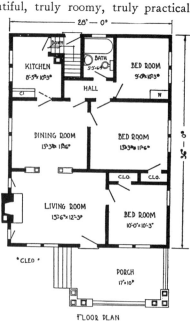

FLOOR PLAN

York

**26 ft. x 34 ft.
over all
5 Rooms and
Bath**

Here is a type of bungalow rightfully popular in the suburban districts of America's big cities. Its general appearance is quite substantial, yet broken roof lines, the careful placing and design of windows, the selection of porch pillars and outside trim give a pleasing balance and harmony one never tires of.

Inside this home you are at once attracted by the warm hospitality of the living room. Two windows at front and side each let in all the sunlight you want. You may have your prized open fireplace; and there's a casement window at the side, underneath which your bookcase may go. Just beyond you catch a glimpse of the dining room. Through a door to the right, but out of sight, are the two bedrooms—one with four windows! There are large closets, a linen closet, and the usual bath. The kitchen is furnished with our celebrated cabinet; a door leads to a grade entrance and to the cellar.

There's a wonderful porch—wide and deep, with room for many a lounging chair, a veranda-swing, or any comfort you may elect.

Owners of the York are most enthusiastic about its individuality, its livableness, its economy both in first and in upkeep cost.

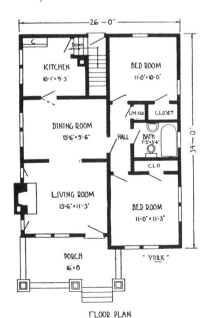

FLOOR PLAN

SPECIFICATIONS

Ceiling height first floor approximately 9 ft.
Girders 6 in. x 8 in.
First floor joists 2 in. x 8 in.
Ceiling joists 2 in. x 4 in. Rafters 2 in. x 6 in.
Front door—our "Conesus," of solid Chestnut, 3 ft. x 6 ft. 8 in. and 1¾ in. thick, glazed with clear glass. *See pages 36–37.*
Prices on oak floors and trim for living room and dining room, maple flooring in kitchen, quoted on application.
Our kitchen cupboard No. 2, medicine cabinet and linen closet included in the selling price. *See pages 36–37.*

See pages 8–9 for general specifications.

¶ IN THE HAPPINESS OF A BENNETT HOME LIES THE HEALTH AND STRENGTH OF THE WHOLE FAMILY.

Salem

**28 ft. x 40 ft.
over all**

**6 Rooms and
Bath**

The Salem seems to fit especially well on a terraced lawn, and its architecture harmonizes well with a "woodsy" setting; or equally well where some of the trees and bushes have been left out of the landscape. To the passerby, this home appears as a rather large and substantial place, the veranda and the main roof gable each lending to this effect. Bracketed and extending eaves add to the beauty of this home. And whether finished with regular siding or shingles, the whole house attracts favorable attention.

One feature is the semi-protection afforded the front entrance to this house. Still another is the possibility of a wonderful fireplace on one end, and underneath casement windows at either side, shelves or cases for your favorite books. There is a pair of charming French doors by which you enter the dining room.

The three sleeping rooms of this home are all arranged on one side—all bright and livable. The bath is separated by entrance into a small private hall. Two of the bedrooms have closets, the third a wardrobe closet; and in addition there is the indispensable linen closet. The kitchen is equipped with a large Bennett Cabinet, and access to outdoors is had through a grade entrance at the rear.

A family who lives in one of the Salems calls it "The best home ever." Perhaps they are prejudiced, but if you owned one we feel certain you, too, would be as enthusiastic over it.

SPECIFICATIONS

Ceiling height first floor approximately 9 ft.
Girders 6 in. x 8 in.
First floor joists 2 in. x 8 in.
Attic joists 2 in. x 6 in. Rafters 2 in. x 6 in.
Front door—our "Mohawk," of solid Chestnut, 3 ft. x 6 ft. 8 in. and 1¾ in. thick, glazed with clear glass.
French doors between living room and dining room.
Prices on oak floors and trim for living room and dining room, maple flooring in kitchen, quoted on application.
Our kitchen cupboard No. 1, medicine cabinet, linen closet, attic stairs and flooring included in the selling price. *See pages 36-37.*
See pages 8-9 for general specifications.

"SALEM" FLOOR PLAN

BED ROOM 11'-0" x 10'-0"
KITCHEN 11'-0" x 9'-3"
CLO.
BED ROOM 11'-0" x 10'-0"
DINING ROOM 11'-11" x 11'-6"
BATH 7'-3"-5'-6"
HALL
CLO.
BED ROOM 11'-0" x 10'-0"
LIVING ROOM 15'-6" x 13'-3"
PORCH 17' x 12'
28'-0"
40'-0"
36'-0"

❡ ARTISTIC DESIGNS WITHOUT INCREASE IN COST IS THE WORK OF BENNETT MASTER ARCHITECTS.

Woodward

26 ft. x 32 ft. over all
5 Rooms and Bath

Inside and outside, common sense is personified in the Woodward—a modest but becoming home which thoroughly expresses that "chummy" spirit which has brought the bungalow into such universal favor. The comfortable atmosphere of the Woodward begins in the spacious porch to which a touch of artistry has been added by the neat colonnades. It's a well-sized, welcoming type of porch which adds to the good appearance of the entire house.

The favorable impression created by the attractive exterior is enhanced as one steps inside. Compactly arranged, but comfortably sized, the entire room scheme provides living, sleeping, eating and all accommodations of sufficient comfort for a family of several persons.

Placing the sleeping rooms on the right side of the house with the day rooms on the left is an appealing plan as it simplifies housework. Both bedrooms have plenty of light and air, while commodious closet space is provided. The bathroom is accessibly located and completes a decidedly practical arrangement.

If the amount of money you have set aside for a home is near the price of the Woodward, you can make it yours with full assurance that its satisfaction will be as great as its economy.

SPECIFICATIONS

Ceiling height first floor approximately 9 ft.
Girders 6 in. x 8 in.
First floor joists 2 in. x 8 in.
Ceiling joists 2 in. x 4 in. Rafters 2 in. x 6 in.
Front door—special design, 3 ft. x 6 ft. 8 in. and 1¾ in. thick.
Our kitchen cupboard No. 2 and medicine cabinet included in the selling price. *See pages 36–37.*

See pages 8–9 for general specifications.

FLOOR PLAN

ONE SHOULD KNOW IN THE BEGINNING WHAT HIS HOME WILL COST IN THE END. YOU ALWAYS DO WHEN BUILDING A BENNETT HOME.

Caledonia, N. Y.
January 18, 1917.

Gentlemen:—
Please send your catalog once in a while. The house I am living in was built with lumber from you, and my wife and I are both well pleased and when I can boost your business I will do it, as a number of persons have asked where I get such good lumber.

Yours truly,
L. F.

Aberdeen

**24 ft. x 32 ft. or
28 ft. x 36 ft. over all
5 Rooms and Bath or
6 Rooms and Bath**

Here is a very smart bungalow that has a host of admirers among our customers. As you look at it from the side view shown here, the things that impress you are the many clever touches to break the straight lines of the home. There is the dormer resting easily on the broad expanse of the front roof. There is the massive chimney at the side, typifying the solidity of this kind of a house. There is the bay window that helps enlarge the dining room. Note particularly that the porch is a part of the house itself, and not merely just "stuck on."

At the front door you are introduced to the comfortable living room, the fireplace at one end, the dining room just beyond. To the left are the two sleeping rooms, both with space aplenty for all usual bedroom furniture.

Please especially note there is a coat closet and a linen closet, a kitchen cabinet, and all the requisites of a well-appointed home.

In Plan "B," we have extended the dimensions to include another bedroom, a closet for each bedroom, and a rear entry-way.

If you are quite taken with the Aberdeen, you will be still more amazed to learn how modest an outlay is required to bring its comforts and conveniences to your fireside.

SPECIFICATIONS

Ceiling height approximately 9 ft.

Floor joists floor plan A 2 in. x 8 in.

Floor joists floor plan B 2 in. x 10 in.

Ceiling joists floor plan A 2 in. x 4 in.

Ceiling joists floor plan B 2 in. x 4 in.

Rafters 2 in. x 6 in.

Front door—our "Mohawk," of solid Chestnut, 3 ft. x 6 ft. 8 in. and 1¾ in. thick, glazed with clear glass.

Cased opening between living room and dining room.

Our kitchen cupboard No. 2 and medicine cabinet included in the selling price, plan A. *See pages 36–37.*

Our kitchen cupboard No. 1 and medicine cabinet included in the selling price, plan B. *See pages 36–37.*

See pages 8–9 for general specifications.

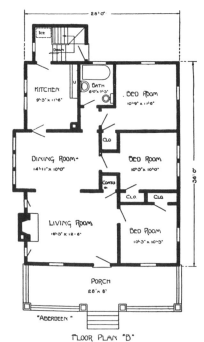

FLOOR PLAN "A"

FLOOR PLAN "B"

Arcadia

**32 ft. x 24 ft.
or 36 ft. x 24 ft.**

5 Rooms and Bath

Nearby this charming Arcadia is another house practically the same size, practically the same cost, yet—you would say the Bennett-Built home is worth all of five hundred dollars more. The increased value is due to clever refinements our architects have given to the Arcadia.

How inviting this home is—and how picturesque with that pergola porch, when in summer, flowering, vines have wound their way around and over it. And let showers come—there is protection from storm and sun while yet enjoying the outdoor breezes on this porch.

But come indoors—Plan "A" first, please. Are you quite fond of a big, hospitable living room—then here you find your wishes realized. Toward the front is the dining room, light and cheerful, with roomy kitchen right behind. On the other side two bedrooms—two windows apiece!—and bathroom between.

But perhaps you would prefer the bedrooms at the back, and closets instead of wardrobes; perhaps you like a practical extension to the kitchen which you have in the back room with its cool place for ice box and its covered way to the cellar—all this and more you will find in "B."

Choose either plan that fits your needs and your tastes best—your choice will delight you many a day to come.

SPECIFICATIONS

Ceiling height first floor approximately 9 ft.

Girders 6 in. x 8 in.

First floor joists 2 in. x 8 in.

Ceiling joists 2 in. x 4 in. Rafters 2 in. x 6 in.

Front door—our "Chautauqua," of solid Chestnut, 3 ft. x 6 ft. 8 in. and 1¾ in. thick, glazed with clear glass.

Our kitchen cupboard No. 1 and medicine cabinet included in the selling price. *See pages 36–37.*

See pages 8–9 for general specifications.

Atherton

28 ft. x 24 ft. over all
6 Rooms and Bath

The Atherton is solid worth from the ground up. There is the delightful spacious porch, the dormer sheltered windows in the sloping roof, the wide eaves that secure graceful lines. And the interior! Seldom do you see so large and lovely a living room—there's the interesting touch of a stairway that wins the heart—a fireplace for snug warmth and hospitality.

You step through a cased opening into the dining room, to find four large windows to assure brightness and cheer. A peep into the convenient, well-lighted kitchen discovers a splendid Bennett kitchen-cupboard.

The upstairs speaks for itself—three large bedrooms and a good-sized bath.

Beautiful—substantial! For people who like to be deeply attached to their home, the Atherton is a real choice.

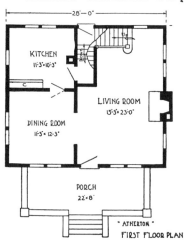

"ATHERTON"
FIRST FLOOR PLAN

SPECIFICATIONS

Ceiling height first floor approximately 9 ft.

Ceiling height second floor approximately 8 ft.

Girders 6 in. x 8 in.

First floor joists 2 in. x 10 in.

Second floor joists 2 in. x 8 in.

Ceiling joists 2 in. x 4 in. Rafters 2 in. x 6 in.

Front door—our "Mohawk," of solid Chestnut, 3 ft. x 6 ft. 8 in. and 1¾ in. thick, glazed with clear glass. *See pages 36–37.*

Prices on oak floors and trim for living room and dining room, maple flooring in kitchen, quoted on application.

Our No. 1 kitchen cupboard, our wardrobe, medicine cabinet and linen closet included in the selling price. *See pages 36–37.*

See pages 8–9 for general specifications.

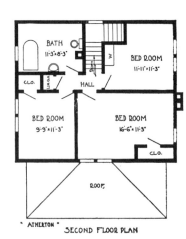

"ATHERTON"
SECOND FLOOR PLAN

APPROVES—WITH NEW ORDER

Gentlemen:—   Moshannon, Pa., May 22, 1919.

Your way of doing fair and square business is perfectly satisfactory. I never used any lumber as near the standard as I get from the Bennett Lumber Co., and I *prove* same in separate envelope *with a nice order.*   C. S. L.

Harriet
28 ft. x 26 ft. over all
6 Rooms and Bath

Here is a home that breathes hospitality. It seems to say "Come in—you'll like living here a long, long while."

You enter the living room—and like it at once. It extends clear across, with a cheery fireplace here and a cozy bay window seat there!

The dining room looms large, well-lighted, with windows carefully placed to accommodate your furniture.

The kitchen, you discover, is bright with light from three windows. You exclaim over the six-foot kitchen cabinet and approve the grade entrance.

Up the stairs you find three large bedrooms with plenty of closet room, a linen closet, and the bathroom *right over the kitchen*, to reduce plumbing costs! Then, last but not least, that big convenience—a large and well-lighted attic.

Sum it up for yourself—"to the very end, the Harriet makes one want to stay."

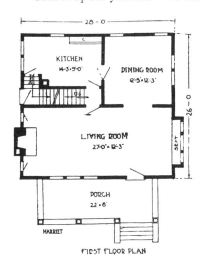

FIRST FLOOR PLAN

SPECIFICATIONS

Ceiling height first floor approximately 9 ft.
Ceiling height second floor approximately 8 ft.
First and second floor joists 2 in. x 8 in.
Attic stairs and attic flooring supported by 2 in. x 6 in. floor joists.
Rafters 2 in. x 6 in.
Front door—our "Mohawk," of solid Chestnut, 3 ft. x 6 ft. 8 in. and 1¾ in. thick, glazed with clear glass. *See pages 36–37.*
Our No. 1 kitchen cabinet, medicine cabinet and linen closet included in selling price.
Window seat in bay.
Prices on oak floors and trim for living room and dining room, maple flooring in kitchen, quoted on application.

See pages 8–9 for general specifications.

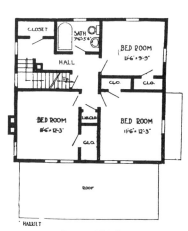

SECOND FLOOR PLAN

Lancaster

**30 ft. x 26 ft. over all
7 Rooms and Bath**

Quiet but rich dignity is this home's expression. The rustic stone chimney and broken ashlar porch wall are most attractive, though brick may be substituted without loss of beauty. The broad, low dormer and wide eaves lend a substantial appearance. The shingled exterior is in keeping with the design; but in case siding is preferred, harmony would not be destroyed.

Off the reception hall is a handy little closet for coats and rubbers. French doors, there are—and a wide fireplace.

See that double swinging door off the kitchen; cupboard in the pantry; direct passage from kitchen through hall to front door. Upstairs—three large bedrooms and closet space aplenty.

For charm, outside and in, and for convenient roominess, the Lancaster is indeed most desirable.

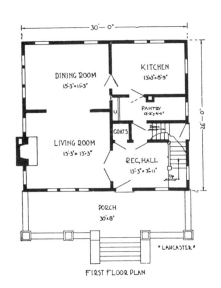

FIRST FLOOR PLAN

SPECIFICATIONS

Ceiling height first floor approximately 9 ft.
Ceiling height second floor approximately 8 ft.
Girders 6 in. x 8 in.
First floor joists 2 in. x 10 in. Second floor joists 2 in. x 8 in.
Ceiling joists 2 in. x 4 in.
Rafters 2 in. x 6 in.
Front door—our "Mohawk," of solid Chestnut, 3 ft. x 6 ft. 8 in. and 1¾ in. thick, glazed with clear glass. *See pages 36–37.*
French doors between living room and reception hall. *See pages 36–37.*
Windows as shown in illustration.
Our No. 2 kitchen cupboard and medicine cabinet included in selling price.
Prices on oak floors and trim in reception hall, living room and dining room, maple flooring in kitchen, quoted on application.

See pages 8–9 for general specifications.

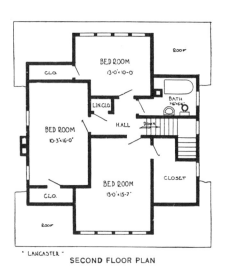

SECOND FLOOR PLAN

Flanders

24 ft. x 22 ft. over all
6 Rooms and Bath

Staunchness is instantly apparent in the practical, good-looking design of the Flanders. You can readily picture this house providing you with all the requirements of modern home-life without burdening you with an investment in unnecessary and costly non-essentials.

Glance at the first floor arrangement and you will see a sensible grouping of all necessary downstairs rooms. There's a tidy hall, with the essential coat closet. The stairway ascends from the right. The living room, bright with light from three broad windows, and another corner room (dining room) furnish an ideal layout.

Coming to the upstairs we will find three thoughtfully proportioned bedrooms, with spacious closet or wardrobe space. The bathroom at the head of the stairs is accessibly located for both floors. For good service you can safely select the Flanders—and in addition secure a genuine bargain.

FIRST FLOOR PLAN

SPECIFICATIONS

Ceiling height first floor approximately 9 ft.

Ceiling height second floor approximately 8 ft.

Girders 6 in. x 8 in.

First and second floor joists 2 in. x 8 in.

Ceiling joists 2 in. x 4 in. Rafters 2 in. x 4 in.

Front door—our "Chautauqua," of solid Chestnut, 3 ft. x 6 ft. 8 in. and 1¾ in. thick, glazed with clear glass. *See pages 36–37.*

Cased opening between living room and dining room.

Our No. 2 kitchen cupboard and medicine cabinet included in the selling price. *See pages 36–37.*

See pages 8–9 for general specifications.

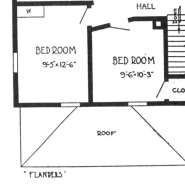

SECOND FLOOR PLAN

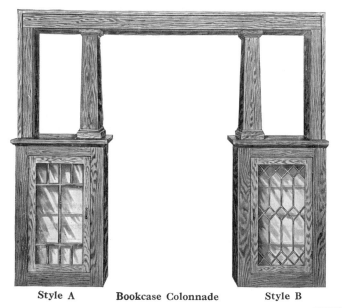

Style A   **Bookcase Colonnade**   Style B

Interior Window

Exterior Window

Stairway

Cottage Door

Medicine Cabinet

Beautiful Graining, Expert Matching, Distinguish These Bennett Articles of Trim

Exterior—Mohawk

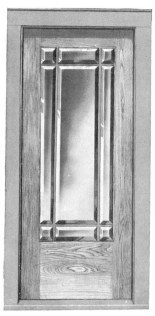

Exterior—Saranac

Exterior—Chautauqua

Exterior—Conesus

36

Niagara Colonnade

Mirror Door

Interior Door

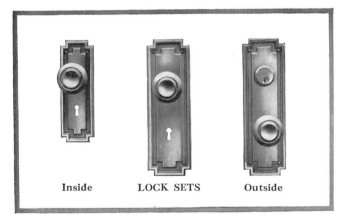

Inside   LOCK SETS   Outside

Linen Closet   **Wardrobe**

French Doors   **Kitchen Cabinet No. 2**   **Kitchen Cabinet No. 1**

Forsyth

36 ft. x 26 ft. over all
8 Rooms and Bath

Here's a design of individuality—practical, substantial.

There's delight upon entering the convenient central hall, to find each room big, airy, inviting.

You peep into the living room to spy casement windows upon either side of a fireplace.

That library! A few Forsyth owners use it as a bedroom by substituting a single door; but most, rejoicing in French doors, never make a change.

There are many conveniences—the large kitchen cabinet, broom closet, the ease of access to all rooms. And see—! Every bedroom on the second floor possesses *two windows* and a closet.

All in all—where could you purchase such splendid architecture and livableness as in this modest-priced Forsyth?

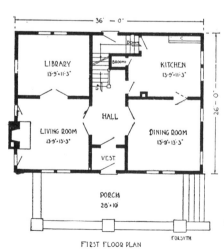

FIRST FLOOR PLAN

SPECIFICATIONS

Ceiling height first floor approximately 9 ft.

Ceiling height second floor approximately 8 ft.

Girders 6 in. x 8 in.

First and second floor joists 2 in. x 10 in.

Ceiling joists 2 in. x 4 in. Rafters 2 in. x 6 in.

Front door—our "Chautauqua," of solid Chestnut, 3 ft. x 6 ft. 8 in. and 1¾ in. thick, glazed with clear glass. *See pages 36–37.*

Vestibule door—our "Chautauqua," of solid Chestnut, 3 ft. x 6 ft. 8 in. and 1¾ in. thick, glazed with clear glass. *See pages 36–37.*

Prices on oak floors and trim in vestibule, hall, living room, library and dining room, maple flooring in kitchen, quoted on application.

Our No. 1 kitchen cupboard, medicine cabinet and linen closet included in selling price.

See pages 8–9 for general specifications.

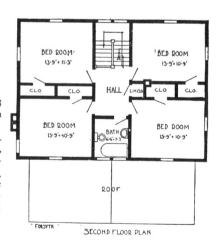

SECOND FLOOR PLAN

Clarendon

**36 ft. x 24 ft. over all
7 Rooms and Bath**

Could you peep through the walls of this Colonial home, you would find yourself regarding an interior as charming as the exterior is picturesque.

But step through that unique latticed entrance and see the house-deep living room—with its hospitable fireplace and casement windows, with nooks for bookcases or built-in seats, and captivating French doors. And what a comfortable lounging place the side veranda furnishes!

French doors upstairs, too, give access from bedrooms to balcony. Note the clever touch in the broken roof lines, increasing the size of the bedrooms—better yet, veritable *sunrooms*.

Be assured this remarkably beautiful home, built the Bennett-Way, is a real dividend-paying investment in beauty, comfort and convenience.

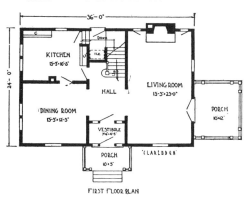

FIRST FLOOR PLAN

SECOND FLOOR PLAN

SPECIFICATIONS

Ceiling height first floor approximately 9 ft.

Ceiling height second floor approximately 8 ft.

Girders 6 in. x 8 in.

First and second floor joists 2 in. x 8 in.

Ceiling joists 2 in. x 4 in. Rafters 2 in. x 4 in.

Front door—Special design of solid Chestnut, 3 ft. x 6 ft. 8 in. and 1¾ in. thick, glazed with clear glass.

Vestibule door, of solid Chestnut, 3 ft. x 6 ft. 8 in. and 1¾ in. thick, glazed with clear glass.

French doors between living room and porch. *See pages 36–37.*

Prices on oak floors and trim in vestibule, hall, living room and dining room, maple flooring in kitchen, quoted on application.

Our No. 1 and No. 2 kitchen cupboards, medicine cabinet and linen closet included in the selling price. *See pages 36–37.*

See pages 8–9 for general specifications.

¶ BENNETT BUILT-IN CONVENIENCES RE-DUCE THE COST OF HOUSE FURNISHING AND INTRODUCE EFFICIENCY INTO THE BUSINESS OF HOUSEKEEPING.

BETTER THAN CLAIMED

Little Valley, N. Y., April 30, 1919.

Gentlemen:—Thank you very much for the honest deal. Everything is okay. Many were sure that I would not get what I ordered, but they were much mistaken. They have seen my lumber and say it is fine, and a number of persons thinking of building said they are going to get their lumber from you.

Yours truly,
J. F. R.

Janis

**28 ft. x 30 ft.
over all**

**8 Rooms and
Bath**

Coziness plus serviceability characterize the Janis—a cozy porch, a complete first floor scheme, and four commodious bedrooms and bath upstairs.

The exposed rafters underneath the roof, the brick chimney, the roof brackets, the clever placing of the trimmings secure an approval for the exterior appearance which is turned to enthusiasm by the attractive rooms within.

One can picture real hospitality in the Janis. The broad, cheerful porch is a fitting introduction to the bright, spacious living room with its welcoming fireplace. The reception hall is an appreciated convenience. French doors between reception hall and living room, and between this last and the dining room add remarkably to the home's smart interior. The dining room has a bay with a tasty window seat. The kitchen is about the same "just right" place as in all our plans. There's a convenient lavatory, too.

The Janis has a well-modeled second floor arrangement. The bedrooms are large-sized and amply proportioned with good light. Three of them are corner rooms.

Choose this home for its ever-attractive styling, the economy of its floor plans, the unique features of its interior—and you will have purchased a thing of permanent pleasure and profit.

SPECIFICATIONS

Ceiling height first floor approximately 9 ft.
Ceiling height second floor approximately 8 ft.
Girders 6 in. x 8 in.
First and second floor joists 2 in. x 8 in.
Ceiling joists 2 in. x 4 in. Rafters 2 in. x 6 in.
Front door—our "Saranac," of solid Chestnut, 3 ft. x 6 ft. 8 in. and 1¾ thick, glazed with clear glass. *See pages 36–37.*
French doors between reception hall and living room; between living room and dining room. *See pages 36–37.*
Prices on oak floors and trim in reception hall, living room and dining room, maple flooring in kitchen, quoted on application.
Our No. 1 kitchen cupboard, medicine cabinet and linen closet included in the selling price. *See pages 36–37.*

See pages 8–9 for general specifications.

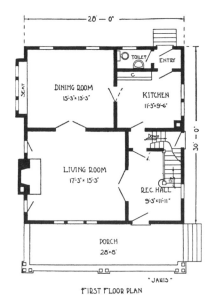

FIRST FLOOR PLAN

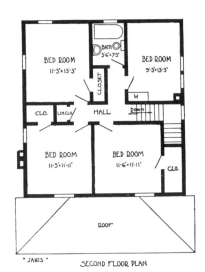

SECOND FLOOR PLAN

Genesee

26 ft. x 24 ft. over all
6 Rooms and Bath

Here's a home that wins wide approval, not so much because it is "the economical square house," but more because it includes decided variations in plan.

For the exterior—the well-placed dormer adds character to the roof. The wide-eaved porch lends dignity to the front. The novel siding supplies individuality.

You are immediately impressed with the roomy living-room—and the fine balance of fireplace at one end and ascending stairway at the other. The dining room is wonderfully cheerful, and with its wide opening to living room is especially prized. The kitchen receives light and air from two sides. The grade entrance saves an extra outside door, yet gives easy access to basement and outdoors.

The bedrooms and the bath all center on an attractive upstairs hall. And see how ample is all closet space. Surely you find every available foot of space utilized to good advantage in this clever "Genesee."

SPECIFICATIONS

Ceiling height first floor approximately 9 ft.

Ceiling height second floor approximately 8 ft.

Girders 6 in. x 8 in.

First and second floor joists 2 in. x 8 in.

Rafters main roof 2 in. x 6 in. Dormer and porch 2 in. x 4 in.

Ceiling joists 2 in. x 4 in.

Front door—our "Mohawk," of solid Chestnut, 3 ft. x 6 ft. 8 in. and 1¾ in. thick, glazed with clear glass. *See pages 36–37.*

Prices on oak floors and trim for living room and dining room, maple flooring in kitchen, quoted on application.

Our No. 1 kitchen cupboard and medicine cabinet included in selling price.

Bungalow siding for exterior.

Windows divided upper sash as shown in illustration.

See pages 8–9 for general specifications.

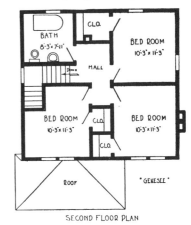

FIRST FLOOR PLAN

KITCHEN
11'-3" x 11'-3"

DINING ROOM
13'-3" x 11'-3"

LIVING ROOM
25'-0" x 11'-3"

PORCH
16' x 7'

" GENESEE "

26' - 0"

24' - 0"

SECOND FLOOR PLAN

BATH
8'-3" x 7'-1"

CLO.

BED ROOM
10'-3" x 11'-3"

HALL

BED ROOM
10'-3" x 11'-3"

CLO.

BED ROOM
10'-3" x 11'-3"

CLO.

ROOF

" GENESEE "

¶ LABOR AND MATERIAL ARE TOO EXPENSIVE TO WASTE. IT DOESN'T PAY TO GUESS AT THE COST OF EITHER. BUY FROM BENNETT AND BE SURE OF YOUR COSTS

NO WASTE

Whippany, N. J., May 22, 1919.

Gentlemen:—I bought lumber of you 25% cheaper than the same quality of goods here. I did not have to throw away any, as I often have to with that bought here.

F. D. J.

Olean

**22 ft. x 26 ft.
over all
6 Rooms and
Bath**

Though somewhat more conservative than others of our two-story designs, the Olean, nevertheless, is dressed with smart lines that lift it out of the ordinary.

The overhanging roof with rafters exposed underneath, the brackets supporting the front, the broad veranda with its stately columns, the placing of the windows and door—all give fine dignity to this home.

On the first floor you find a rather generous living room; stairs on one side, two pleasant windows opposite and a wide opening leading to the square dining room, made pleasant by light from two sides. The kitchen is set by itself, and access to the side entrance and the cellar is gained through a compact and serviceable entry.

On the second floor there is one quite remarkable bedroom, and two others of just the right size. The usual bath is found near the bedrooms. Especially, notice the triple windows in the large bedroom and the extra large closet that room boasts.

The modest investment required in the Olean represents, we believe, a home value second to none.

SPECIFICATIONS

Ceiling height first floor approximately 9 ft.

Ceiling height second floor approximately 8 ft.

Girders 6 in. x 8 in.

First and second floor joists 2 in. x 8 in.

Ceiling joists 2 in. x 4 in.   Rafters 2 in. x 4 in.

Front door—our "Conesus," of solid Chestnut, 3 ft. x 6 ft. 8 in. and 1¾ in. thick, glazed with clear glass. *See pages 36–37.*

Wardrobe in two rear bedrooms.

Our kitchen cupboard No. 1 and medicine cabinet included in the selling price. *See pages 36–37.*

See pages 8–9 for general specifications.

FIRST FLOOR PLAN

22'-0"

26'-0"

KITCHEN
9'-5"x 11'-5"

DINING ROOM
11'-5"x 11'-5"

C

DOWN

LIVING ROOM
21'-0"x 13'-5"

PORCH
18' x 8'

"OLEAN"

SECOND FLOOR PLAN

W

BED ROOM
9'-9" x 11'-5"

BED ROOM
10'-9"x 8'-5"

BATH
7'-5"x 5'-10"

HALL

DOWN

CLO.

BED ROOM
17'-5"x 10'-0"

ROOF

"OLEAN"

Hartley

24 ft. x 28 ft. over all
6 Rooms, Bath,
Sleeping Porch

If a family's choice leans toward the "square" house, it is fairly certain that the Hartley will be one of those seriously considered—for in it a rare degree of appearance, livableness, and economy of plan have been combined.

The front of this home is quite impressive. To begin with, there's a porch embracing the entire width of the house. Its gently sloping roof blends in with the shingle covered second story. Broad top roofs, front and sides, are adequately broken with wide dormers, giving a final touch to an exterior already most attractive.

As you enter the reception hall a pretty stairway leads up to the half-way landing. Directly ahead is one of those highly desirable conveniences, a coat closet. Then, through a wide opening, you are greeted by a sight of a rather large living room —the bright dining room just beyond adding its share to the home's invitation. The kitchen is replete with both cabinet and pantry! There is a rear and a side entrance, the last at grade.

We will let the three fine bedrooms, the big closets, tell their own story—and pass the bath with just the name of it, but—here is something to talk about, an outdoor sleeping place! There's a real treat for some of the family in that feature—who will the lucky ones be?

For the "right" kind of a home, at the "right" kind of a price—consider thoughtfully the Hartley.

SPECIFICATIONS

Ceiling height first floor approximately 9 ft.
Ceiling height second floor approximately 8 ft.
Girders 6 in. x 8 in.
First and second floor joists 2 in. x 8 in.
Attic joists 2 in. x 6 in. Rafters 2 in. x 6 in.
Front door—our "Mohawk," of solid Chestnut, 3 ft. x 6 ft. 8 in. and 1¾ in. thick, glazed with clear glass. *See pages 36–37.*
Prices on oak floors and trim in hall, living room and dining room, maple flooring in kitchen, quoted on application.
Our No. 2 kitchen cupboard and medicine cabinet included in the selling price. *See pages 36–37.*
Attic stairs and flooring included in selling price.

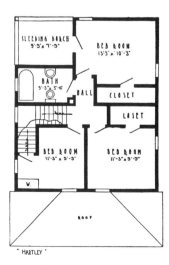

See pages 8–9 for general specifications.

43

Colonial

38 ft. x 26 ft.
7 Rooms and Bath

Here's a masterpiece in designing—both for beauty of exterior and for ideal arrangement. This house faithfully reproduces the atmosphere of Colonial days, yet with touches of modernism which have been tried and approved by best architectural practice.

Perhaps the first unique thing you notice are the seats at either side of the doorway—then the quaint Colonial door with its narrow side windows. As the door swings back you are welcomed, through French doors, to a magnificent living room, fireplace at the farther end, and built-in bookcases underneath pretty casement windows. Through the door or window at the right of the room you spy the privacy of a well-sheltered porch.

Just in front of you the stairway leads straight to the second story. Through another pair of French doors, you note the dining room. At the rear of the hall is a convenient lavatory and underneath the stairs a very useful coat closet.

As you notice the corner location of each bedroom, and the large closets in each, stop a passing minute in the rear bedroom at the right to see that you may have a fireplace here, too.

The Colonial is a design quite beyond the ordinary for a cost quite less than ordinary. Does it suit your needs?—Then write us for more definite information.

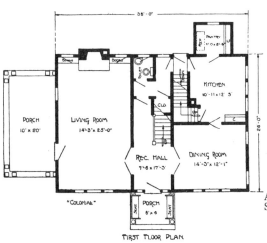

FIRST FLOOR PLAN

SPECIFICATIONS

Ceiling height first floor approximately 9 ft.
Ceiling height second floor approximately 8 ft.
Girders 6 in. x 8 in.
First and second floor joists 2 in. x 10 in.
Attic joists 2 in. x 6 in.
Rafters 2 in. x 6 in.
Front door—as illustrated, 3 ft. x 6 ft. 8 in. and 1¾ in. thick.
French doors between hall and living room, also between hall and dining room.
Bookcase on each side of fireplace.
Prices on oak floors and trim in hall, living room and dining room, maple flooring in kitchen, quoted on application.
Pantry and kitchen cabinets furnished in Yellow Pine.
Attic stairs and flooring included in the selling price.
Seats for front entrance included in the selling price.

See pages 8–9 for general specifications.

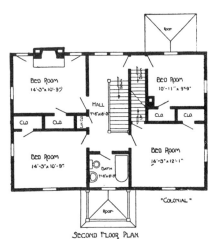

SECOND FLOOR PLAN

44

Erie

24 ft. x 26 ft. over all

6 Rooms, Bath, Hall

However much house styles may change, that most practical of all plans, the square house, always remains in vogue. And "The Erie" is genuinely an all-prized design of this most popular type.

There is a prosperous, substantial appearance to this home. It is free from elaboration—yet full of the spice of style. The extending roof with its distinctive dormer, the shingled upper story, the wide expanse of porch, the solid type of porch pillars—everything bears out the impression that here live people of a most desirable American type. The first room inside is a reception hall, serving the purpose of receiving the casual caller, and of providing the place from whence a simple stairway winds toward the upstairs. The living room is a square one with five windows to guarantee a flood of light. From here a colonnade-opening leads to the dining room on one of the back corners of the house. This room is also bright with light. The kitchen is the usual compact and complete Bennett arrangement. There is a passageway from the kitchen to the front hall.

The upstairs arrangement of this home is as ideal as that of the lower floor—every room a corner room. Three spacious sleeping chambers—each with its own capacious closet—a convenient bath and a handy linen closet complete the layout.

"The Erie," outside and inside, is a most inviting home—its arrangement is most practical and most complete—its construction and finish of a quiet, rich and enduring type.

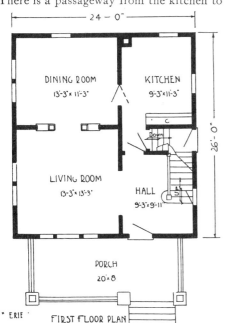

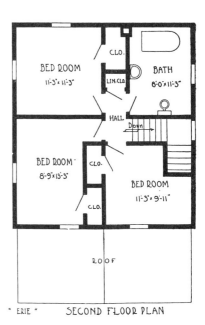

SPECIFICATIONS

Ceiling height first floor approximately 9 ft.
Ceiling height second floor approximately 8 ft.
Girders 6 in. x 8 in.
First and second floor joists 2 in. x 8 in.
Ceiling joists 2 in. x 4 in. Rafters 2 in. x 6 in.
Front door—our "Chautauqua," of solid Chestnut, 3 ft. x 6 ft. 8 in. and 1¾ in. thick, glazed with clear glass. *See pages 36–37.*
"Niagara" colonnade between living room and dining room. *See pages 36–37.*
Our No. 1 kitchen cupboard, medicine cabinet and linen closet included in selling price. *See pages 36–37.*

See pages 8–9 for general specifications.

Frederick

24 ft. x 42 ft. over all
Two-Family Dwelling
5 Rooms, Bath—Each

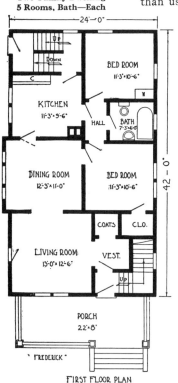

FIRST FLOOR PLAN

It is a thrifty family who, in building its own home, provides for a tenant to pay taxes and upkeep and, besides, a comfortable profit. To such a family, the Frederick has much to recommend it. Red Cedar Shingle and Redwood clapboard side wall protection has been provided to give more than usual character to the design, and lasting life. The spacious substantial porches provide outdoor comfort for both families. The whole exterior is one of fine balance and dignity.

Upstairs and down the living rooms are ample, attractive, a casement window enriching each; just back are the dining rooms with three splendid windows apiece. Airy, light kitchens connect through double swinging doors. There's a back entryway with room for the refrigerator. On the other side of the house are the two bedrooms—two windows apiece—with bath just between. There are coat closets, clothes closets, medicine and kitchen cabinets, and wardrobes to satisfy every need. And last but not least—you may make extra rooms in the attic.

SPECIFICATIONS

Ceiling height first floor approximately 9 ft.
Ceiling height second floor approximately 9 ft.
Girders 6 in. x 8 in.
First and second floor joists 2 in. x 8 in.
Ceiling joists 2 in. x 6 in. Rafters 2 in. x 6 in.
Front door—our "Saranac," of solid Chestnut, 3 ft. x 6 ft. 8 in. and 1¾ in. thick, glazed with clear glass. *See pages 36–37.*
Prices on oak floors and trim in hall, living room and dining room, maple flooring in kitchen, quoted on application.
Wardrobes in rear bedrooms.
Our kitchen cupboards No. 1 and medicine cabinets included in the selling price. *See pages 36–37.*

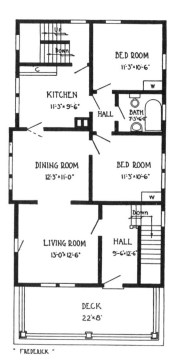

SECOND FLOOR PLAN

See pages 8–9 for general specifications.

Nelson

24 ft. x 36 ft. over all
5 Rooms, Bath, Hall

There is fine simplicity in the Nelson. Here is a dwelling-place to satisfy exacting tastes for a refined home of modest proportions.

One likes the clean-cut columns and railing on the friendly porch—the exposed rafters—the well-proportioned dormers.

The ample-sized rooms are expressly planned for a wealth of sunshine, yet with sufficient wall-space for placement of furniture.

Conveniences! Note the coat closet—the hall affording privacy to the bath—the ideal location of the kitchen cupboard for simplified serving. There's a pretty cased arch between living and dining room, and between hall and living room.

A sound purchase—if you wish beauty, comfort and durability—is the substantial Nelson.

SPECIFICATIONS

Ceiling height first floor approximately 9 ft.
Girders 6 in. x 8 in.
First floor joists 2 in. x 8 in.
Ceiling joists 2 in. x 4 in. Rafters 2 in. x 6 in.
Front door—our "Conesus," of solid Chestnut, 3 ft. x 6 ft. 8 in. and 1¾ in. thick, glazed with clear glass. *See pages 36–37.*
Our No. 2 kitchen cupboard, wardrobe and medicine cabinet included in the selling price. *See pages 36–37.*

See pages 8–9 for general specifications.

BY BUYING ALL MATERIAL FROM ONE CONCERN THE BLAME FOR DELAYS AND SHORTAGES, IF ANY, CAN BE PLACED WHERE IT JUSTLY BELONGS. SEE THE BENNETT GUARANTEE.

Richard

26 ft. x 34 ft. over all
5 Rooms and Bath

In the Richard, the keynote in architecture and arrangement alike, is Utility. Day-by-day usefulness has been built into each unit of its construction from the pleasant porch to the much-used storeroom on the second floor.

This house has been created to accommodate a small family with modest needs and tastes. But if more bed rooms are required, two large comfortable well lighted rooms with closets may be secured on the second floor at a nominal expense. Stairs leading from dining room and matched flooring for entire second floor are included in selling price.

Like all Bennett-Built Homes, the Richard has well-lighted and well-proportioned rooms without an exception. There has been incorporated every advantage of a costly home, built on a basis of strictest economy.

It is a substantial, durable, dependable house that embodies every vital feature for a happy home within the means of a moderate income.

SPECIFICATIONS

Ceiling height first floor approximately 9 ft.

Girders 6 in. x 8 in.

First floor joists 2 in. x 8 in.

Ceiling joists 2 in. x 6 in.   Rafters 2 in. x 6 in.

Front door—glazed cottage design, 3 ft. x 6 ft. 8 in. and 1¾ in. thick. *See pages 36–37.*

Our No. 2 kitchen cupboard and medicine cabinet included in the selling price. *See pages 36–37.*

See pages 8–9 for general specifications.

FLOOR PLAN B

> Emporium, Pa.
> *Gentlemen:—*   May 20, 1919.
> The material furnished me was as good as I expected it to be. And as near as I could estimate, think the price was at least 20% cheaper delivered here than I could have bought the same grade of material from our local dealers.   M. F. L.

> Upland, Pa.
> *Gentlemen:—*   May 10, 1919.
> I received my lumber all O. K. several days ago and have just finished working with it. I must say that I was more than pleased with it. It was all perfect goods.
>   C. N. H.

> Lockport, N. Y.
> *Gentlemen:—*   May 20, 1919.
> I am perfectly satisfied with the quality of your lumber. Your prices are enough lower so I can save from one to two hundred dollars on a house bill, which is an item any contractor should consider.
>   C. T. N.

Rochester

22 ft. x 32 ft. over all
7 Rooms and Bath

Charm has been our watchword in the creation of the Rochester—a charming exterior as well as a charming room arrangement. A house of modest proportions at moderate cost has been attained without sacrificing either inside or outside attractiveness.

The sloping roof lines blend in gracefully with the shingled walls and the veranda. Entering the home, one finds a living room indeed luxurious for a home of this size. A dandy dining room and the usual kitchen, together with a secluded den, complete the first floor layout.

Upstairs, three bedrooms, each large and double-windowed and furnished with roomy closets, and the bath are the remaining details that combine to make the Rochester a home of great popularity. Interested?—then we would like to send you *all* the good news about it—write.

SPECIFICATIONS

Ceiling height first floor approximately 9 ft.

Ceiling height second floor approximately 8 ft.
    Ceiling slightly hipped.

Girders 6 in. x 8 in.

First and second floor joists 2 in. x 8 in.

Ceiling joists 2 in. x 4 in.

Rafters 2 in. x 6 in.

Front door as illustrated, 3 ft. x 6 ft. 8 in. and 1¾ in. thick, glazed with clear glass.

Our No. 1 kitchen cupboard and medicine cabinet included in the selling price. *See pages 36–37.*

See pages 8–9 for general specifications.

FIRST FLOOR PLAN

- 22'—0"
- PORCH 10'·6'
- DEN 11'-3"x8'-9
- KITCHEN 9'-3"x9'-11
- DINING ROOM 11'-3"x10'-0"
- 32'—0"
- LIVING ROOM 21'-0"x11'-3"
- PORCH 17'x8'
- "ROCHESTER"

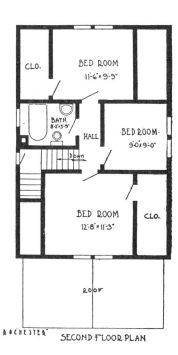

SECOND FLOOR PLAN

- CLO.
- BED ROOM 11'-6"x9'-9"
- BATH 8'-2"x5'-5"
- HALL
- BED ROOM 9'-0"x9'-0"
- BED ROOM 12'-8"x11'-3"
- CLO.
- ROOF
- "ROCHESTER"

Dover

26 ft. x 36 ft. over all
6 Rooms and Bath

The Dover is a splendid example of how the all-on-one-floor bungalow home can luxuriously and comfortably house a large family.

In appearance, this home is ideally balanced. Graceful roof lines blend into its shingled sides. Porch pillars carry through the idea of substantiality. Overhanging eaves give the final touch to the bungalow theme.

Let us analyze the Dover from the viewpoint of solid comfort. The twenty-six foot porch promises plenty of outdoor comfort and air. The living room provides space for not only the whole family but several guests in addition. The dining room is large enough to accommodate a holiday dinner party. In case of large entertainments, the two rooms can practically be opened into one. The three bedrooms suffice for a family of five or six—or with less people, a guest room is available.

There's a kitchen ample for all needs.

You may have noticed where you can build a fireplace in the living room. That bay in the dining room you can plan for flowers and plants, or just a cozy cushioned seat. You have made a note of that celebrated step-saver, the kitchen cabinet. Did you see the closets for each sleeping room?

If it's a bungalow home that meets your fondest wishes, and the Dover satisfies your needs, then we can assure you that it will be ideal.

SPECIFICATIONS

Ceiling height first floor approximately 9 ft.
Girders 6 in. x 8 in.
First floor joists 2 in. x 8 in.
Ceiling joists 2 in. x 4 in.   Rafters 2 in. x 6 in.
Ceiling joists plan B 2 in. x 6 in.
Front door—special design, 3 ft. x 6 ft. 8 in. and
    1¾ in. thick, glazed.
French doors between living room and dining room.
Our kitchen cupboard No. 2 and medicine cabinet
    included in the selling price. *See pages 36–37.*
Attic stairs and flooring included in the selling price
    of plan B.

See pages 8–9 for general specifications.

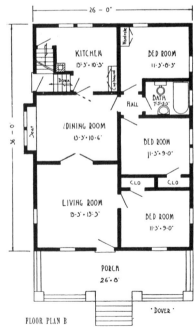

FLOOR PLAN

FLOOR PLAN B

Sherrill

**22 ft. x 32 ft. or
24 ft. x 36 ft. over all
6 Rooms and Bath or
5 Rooms and Bath**

The Sherrill is a home of snug contentment—the type of home that will nestle alongside a country road or adorn a city street, presenting a charming appearance anywhere.

The broad porch, dormer window and graceful roof make an unusually pleasing exterior. The profile or side view is equally interesting. For the interior arrangement, two alternate plans are offered. The one provides three bedrooms, the other two. Living, dining room, kitchen and bath are found in generous size in both. A wide opening between living and dining room in each case provides an advantageous feature for "affairs." Select the plan you prefer—either one will provide you with a lifetime service of true satisfaction.

SPECIFICATIONS

PLAN A
Ceiling height first floor approximately 9 ft.
Girders 6 in. x 8 in.
First floor joists 2 in. x 8 in. Rafters 2 in. x 4 in.
Front door—our "Mohawk," of solid Chestnut, 3 ft.
x 6 ft. 8 in. and 1¾ in. thick, glazed with
clear glass.
Cased opening between living room and dining room.
Our kitchen cupboard No. 1 included in the selling
price. *See pages 36–37.*

PLAN B
Ceiling height first floor approximately 9 ft.
Girders 6 in. x 8 in.
First floor joists 2 in. x 8 in. Rafters 2 in. x 6 in.
Front door—our "Mohawk," of solid Chestnut, 3 ft.
x 6 ft. 8 in. and 1¾ in. thick, glazed with
clear glass.
Cased opening between living room and dining room.
Wardrobe in rear bedroom.
Our kitchen cupboard No. 2 included in the selling
price. *See pages 36–37.*

See pages 8–9 for general specifications.

FLOOR PLAN "A"

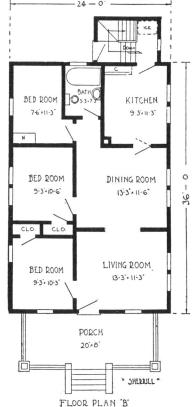

FLOOR PLAN "B"

Maidstone
**22 ft. x 26 ft. or
22 ft. x 30 ft. over all
5 Rooms and Bath—
or just 4 Rooms**

"Be it ever so humble, there's no place like home"—might well have been written with this cosy cottage in mind. Though quite humble, the Maidstone is decidedly "homey".

Most houses of a like size are usually quite ugly—but see how a bracketed roof, cleverly shingled side walls, and the artistic use of exterior trim, transforms this Bennett-Built Cottage into a really attractive home.

But now let's look indoors—into the smaller plan, first. For simple purposes, can you conceive a simpler layout? Just two partitions, and you have—living and dining room, kitchen, and two bedrooms.

But some families desire a bit different arrangement, a separate dining room, and a bath. There you find it in Plan "B"— with a closed back entry thrown in for good measure. And notice the sheltered porch, whichever plan you favor.

If the Maidstone fills your needs, the satisfaction you will find living in it will be as great as your surprise at its low cost.

SPECIFICATIONS

Ceiling height first floor approximately 8 ft. 6 in.
Girders 6 in. x 8 in.
First floor joists 2 in. x 8 in.
Ceiling joists 2 in. x 4 in. Rafters 2 in. x 4 in.
Front door—our glazed cottage design, 2 ft. 8 in. x 6 ft. 8 in. and 1¾ in. thick. *See pages 36–37.*
Our kitchen cupboard No. 2 and medicine cabinet included in the selling price. (Plan B.) *See pages 36–37.*
Our kitchen cupboard No. 2 included in the selling price. (Plan A.) *See pages 36–37.*
(If basement is not wanted in Plan B, omit rear addition and basement stairs, saving in price.)

See pages 8–9 for general specifications.

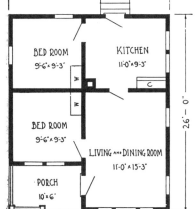

FLOOR PLAN "A"

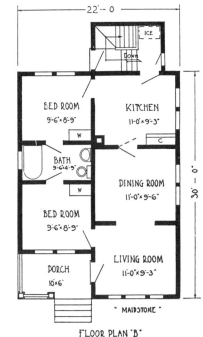

FLOOR PLAN "B"

Lawton

**24 ft. x 30 ft. or
24 ft. x 36 ft. over all
5 Rooms, Bath or
6 Rooms, Bath**

Simplicity is in the keynote of this cottage home—a simplicity, however, enriched by clever lines of roof, porch and whole-house architecture.

Plan "A" provides for a moderate-sized family—a cheerful, roomy living room, rather good-sized dining room and a compact, convenient kitchen. The bedrooms contain room aplenty for bed, dresser and other bedroom furnishings; and, of course, there is the very necessary bath. In "B" there's an additional bedroom for the family of larger numbers. In addition there are closets off the sleeping rooms. The kitchen and bath are differently located—the dining room is slightly increased to accommodate the larger number of persons.

You will agree, we are confident, that for compact design, yet plenty of room to keep out of each other's way, either of the two Lawton plans offers a most pleasing choice.

SPECIFICATIONS

Ceiling height first floor approximately 9 ft.

Girders 6 in. x 8 in.

First floor joists 2 in. x 8 in.

Ceiling joists 2 in. x 4 in. Rafters 2 in. x 6 in.

Front door—our "Conesus," of solid Chestnut, 3 ft. x 6 ft. 8 in. and 1¾ in. thick, glazed with clear glass. *See pages 36–37.*

Our kitchen cupboard No. 2 and medicine cabinet included in the selling price. *See pages 36–37.*

Price on rear addition and basement stairs same as shown with Maidstone, plan B, quoted on application.

See pages 8–9 for general specifications.

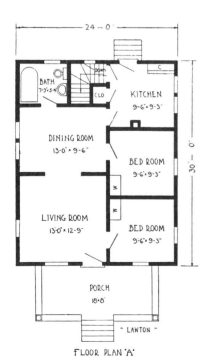

FLOOR PLAN "A"

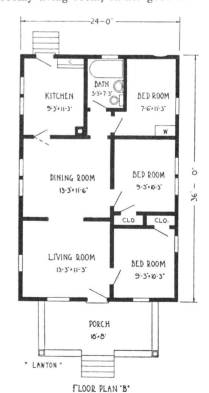

FLOOR PLAN "B"

Kenmore

**20 ft. x 18 ft. or
24 ft. by 20 ft. over all
3 or 4 Rooms**

The one best way to prove a home's worth is by the testimony of those who have lived in it. By such people the Kenmore is classified as a "snug, perfect little place."

We need not dwell at length on the exterior, for you can see what goes to make it up.

The interior is as easy to understand, too. The living room is of unusual size for such a kind of home. The single bedroom has light and air from two sides, and to save extra cost, we included our wardrobe clothes closet. In the kitchen, again to save extra cost, we have included our cabinet.

In Plan "B," we have provided an extra bedroom and quite sizable closets, leaving the living room with space aplenty, and having added enough room in the kitchen so that the family may eat at a table over in the corner.

There is a lot to say about the economy of either Kenmore. But let the price of it argue for itself. If it suits you, we can fill your order in a few hours.

SPECIFICATIONS

Ceiling height first floor approximately 9 ft.

Girders 6 in. x 6 in.

First floor joists 2 in. x 8 in.

Ceiling joists 2 in. x 4 in. Rafters 2 in. x 4 in.

Front door—glazed cottage design, 3 ft. x 6 ft. 8 in. and 1¾ in. thick. See pages 36-37.

Our kitchen cupboard No. 2 included in the selling price. See pages 36-37.

See pages 8-9 for general specifications.

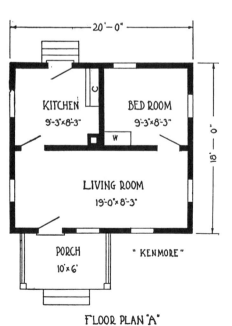

FLOOR PLAN "A"

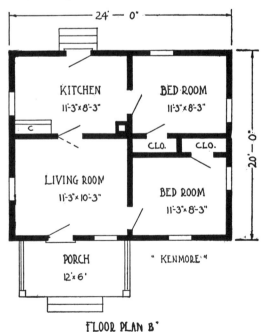

FLOOR PLAN "B"

Cloverdale

20 ft. x 30 ft. or
22 ft. x 30 ft. over all
5 Rooms alone or
5 Rooms and Bath

Of all tidy, economical cottages, its friends vote "The Cloverdale" ideal—most wholesome. Though covering only 600 sq. ft., the proportions of length, width and height have been admirably balanced, and a neat porch added. Notice the bracketed roof, exposed rafter ends, extending porch roof with richly shaped pillars, windows and door nicely balancing the whole front.

In plan "A," there's a most restful living room with one end for a cozy fireside. A wide opening leads to an ideal dining room. The kitchen, directly back, contains our labor-saving cabinet. The two bedrooms are practically alike, both well lighted, well aired and provided with wardrobes, giving all the convenience of regular closets.

In "B," by adding two feet to the width and saving a bit on the living room, we have slightly enlarged the dining room and made the plan complete with snug bath and fine pantry. The bedrooms, too, are slightly larger.

SPECIFICATIONS

Ceiling height first floor approximately 9 ft.
Plan A girders 6 in. x 6 in.; Plan B girders 6 in. x 8 in.
First floor joists 2 in. x 8 in.
Ceiling joists 2 in. x 4 in. Rafters 2 in. x 4 in.
Front door—glazed cottage design, 2 ft. 8 in. x 6 ft. 8 in. *See pages 36–37.*
Our No. 2 kitchen cupboard included in the selling price, Plan A. *See pages 36–37.*
Our No. 2 kitchen cupboard and medicine cabinet included in the selling price, Plan B. *See pages 36–37.*
Price on rear addition and basement stairs same as shown with Maidstone, plan B, page 52, quoted on application.

See pages 8–9 for general specifications.

FLOOR PLAN "A"

BED ROOM
8'-5" x 9'-3"

KITCHEN
9'-9" x 9'-3"

BED ROOM
8'-9" x 9'-6"

DINING ROOM
9'-9" x 9'-6"

LIVING ROOM
15'-0" x 9'-3"

PORCH
19' x 7'

"CLOVERDALE"

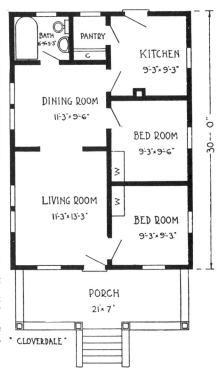

FLOOR PLAN "B"

BATH
6'-5" x 5'-3"

PANTRY

KITCHEN
9'-3" x 9'-3"

DINING ROOM
11'-3" x 9'-6"

BED ROOM
9'-3" x 9'-6"

LIVING ROOM
11'-3" x 13'-3"

BED ROOM
9'-3" x 9'-3"

PORCH
21' x 7'

"CLOVERDALE"

Auburn

**20 ft. x 28 ft. or
22 ft. x 30 ft. over all
4 Rooms and Bath or
5 Rooms and Bath**

For rock-bottom economy, we know of no "buy" that betters the Auburn. Though minus the comfort of a roof over porch, this home does include a place to enjoy the outdoor air. Overhanging roof, shingled sides, and a clever handling of the windows and doors gives the Auburn a smart effect not found in the common house of this type.

For economy of space and work, the living and dining room have been combined in plan "A," but space has not been sacrificed in the sizable kitchen, nor has closet room been overlooked in either of the bedrooms.

In plan "B," the house dimensions have been slightly increased to secure a separation of living room from dining room, and the addition of a pantry off of the kitchen. A slight enlargement of the bedrooms was also possible—especially since wardrobes could satisfactorily take the place of closets.

Could you see this home as it actually exists and compare its appearance and finish, outside and in, with others of the same type, you would not hesitate a minute in choosing the Auburn—further, a comparison of costs would confirm your selection.

SPECIFICATIONS

Ceiling height first floor approximately 8 ft. 6 in.
Girders 6 in. x 6 in.
First floor joists 2 in. x 8 in.
Ceiling joists 2 in. x 4 in. Rafters 2 in. x 4 in.
Front door— our Glazed Cottage design, 2 ft. 8 in. x 6 ft. 8 in. *See pages 36–37.*
Our kitchen cupboard No. 2 and medicine cabinet included in the selling price. *See pages 36–37.*
Price on rear addition and basement stairs as shown with Shamrock, plan B, page 57, quoted on application.

See pages 8–9 for general specifications.

FLOOR PLAN "A"

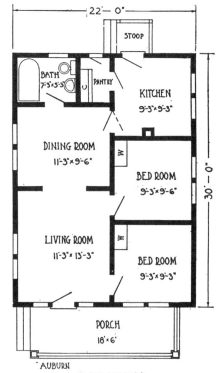

FLOOR PLAN "B"

Shamrock

**22 ft. x 26 ft. or 30 ft. over all
Five Rooms and Bath or
Four Rooms**

Here is a solid, substantial, livable type of cottage home—a dwelling not only well-built, but also most convenient and comfortable.

The Shamrock provides all of the essentials of an attractive exterior without expensive and unnecessary frills and innovations. Yet there are snappy touches of design—bracket-supported roof, exposed rafter, combined shingle and regular siding effects—to differentiate this home from the ordinary.

You will observe that you can have your choice of two floor plans. Plan "B" includes a connecting bathroom which is eliminated in "A," as that plan is designed for localities where sewerage connections are not available. Plan "A" also extends the living room to include the dining accommodations, making possible a four-foot contraction in the depth of the house, and thus a substantial saving in cost.

The porch is ample and well protected. The rooms are fairly proportioned and well lighted. Note the convenient built-in wardrobes in the good-sized bedrooms, and the additional rear room (or summer kitchen) provided in "B."

Either plan will provide you with a satisfying, serviceable home—for an investment that is decidedly modest.

SPECIFICATIONS

Ceiling height first floor approximately 8 ft. 6 in.
Girders 6 in. x 6 in.
First floor joists 2 in. x 8 in.
Ceiling joists 2 in. x 4 in. Rafters 2 in. x 4 in.
Front door—glazed cottage design, 2 ft. 8 in. x 6 ft. 8 in. and 1¾ in. thick. *See pages 36–37.*
Wardrobes in bedrooms.
Our kitchen cupboard No. 2 included in the selling price. *See pages 36–37.*

See pages 8–9 for general specifications.

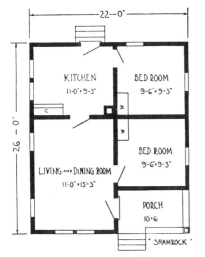

FLOOR PLAN "A"

FLOOR PLAN "B"

Delaware

30 ft. x 26 ft. or 34 ft. x 24 ft.
5 Rooms and Bath

Here's a cottage bidding for your favor not merely because of its modest building cost, but also because of unique beauty and balance of design—nothing overdone, and nothing forgotten. Notice how this compact little home invites approval with its graceful overhanging eaves, the individuality of its half-siding and half-shingle exterior, and its broad, roomy porch.

And inside! Two rooms on the front—both the large living room and the cozy dining room! In Plan "A" notice especially the well-located pantry; and the hall giving privacy to bedrooms and bath. In Plan "B" see that convenient bathroom arrangement, and the kitchen made roomier, the pantry room cared for in this plan by one of our efficient kitchen cabinets.

In both plans you find the same serviceable refrigerator location, and side and back entrance combined in one—with the cellar easily reached by a few steps.

Comparing all—where can you find more distinctive appearance, more compact utility than in this "homey" little Delaware?

SPECIFICATIONS

Ceiling height first floor approximately 9 ft.

Girders 6 in. x 8 in.

First floor joists 2 in. x 8 in.

Ceiling joists 2 in. x 4 in. Rafters 2 in. x 6 in.

Front door—our "Mohawk," of solid Chestnut, 3 ft. x 6 ft. 8 in. and 1¾ in. thick, glazed with clear glass.

Our kitchen cupboard No. 2 and medicine cabinet included in the selling price. *See pages 36–37.*

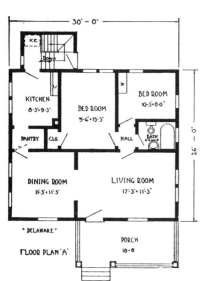

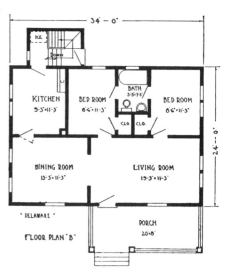

See pages 8–9 for general specifications.

58

Monroe

30 ft. x 32 ft. over all
5 Rooms and Bath

The all-in-one floor scheme of bungalow-homes is quite as much in their favor as their comparatively modest cost—from both viewpoints the Monroe is a faithful example of this design.

There's an air of stability to this home—solidity and endurance, yet not a bit overdone. And notice the harmony of roof lines; the extending and protecting eaves, with rafter ends just showing here and there. And if you like them better, shingled side walls in soft-toned colors might be used, certainly with no loss of effect.

Perhaps a most striking feature of the interior is its large inviting living room, with a truly pleasant dining room just to the right—a wide opening between, a decided advantage when entertaining. And do not overlook the kitchen's easy access to cellar, to entry and sheltered back porch. The lady of the home will be glad to see that handy linen closet; to especially mark the cheerful bedrooms, and their ample closet space.

What more of convenience, of roomy compactness could be asked in this home—what better dollar-for-dollar value.

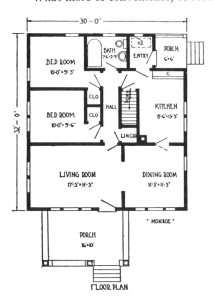

FLOOR PLAN

SPECIFICATIONS

Ceiling height first floor approximately 9 ft.

Girders 6 in. x 8 in.

First floor joists 2 in. x 8 in.

Ceiling joists 2 in. x 4 in.   Rafters 2 in. x 6 in.

Front door—our "Mohawk," of solid Chestnut, 3 ft. x 6 ft. 8 in. and 1¾ in. thick, glazed with clear glass.

Prices on oak floors and trim for living room and dining room, maple flooring in kitchen, quoted on application.

Our kitchen cupboard No. 1, medicine cabinet and linen closet included in the selling price. *See pages 36–37.*

See pages 8–9 for general specifications.

> ❡ IT IS NEVER THE SIZE OF A HOME THAT MAKES IT ATTRACTIVE, BUT THE CARE WITH WHICH IT IS DESIGNED AND KEPT.

Freeport, Pa., May 20, 1919.

Gentlemen:—
    All lumber in fine condition, and better than we had expected. Claim to have *saved $300.* Your business methods were most satisfactory to us.

Yours truly,

J. A. McE.

Beverly

20 ft. x 28 ft. or 30 ft.
over all
5 Rooms or 4 Rooms
and Bath

This sturdy, practical, pleasing home offers everything to be desired in comfortable living quarters, while reducing the cost of home-building to a most moderate basis.

Notice, please, the novel hooded type of porch, the bevel glass door, the general tidy appearance of the whole front.

Observe the choice of two floor plans; the bathroom being omitted in "A," but an extra sleeping chamber being gained. Both plans provide the same splendid house-wide living room, sizable dining room and kitchen; both include an efficient kitchen cabinet; both provide ample clothes-keeping facilities in the shape of large wardrobes.

You can choose whichever plan is most suited to your conditions with the certainty that you are selecting a home that embodies both economy and service in the highest sense.

SPECIFICATIONS

PLAN A—
Ceiling height first floor approximately 8 ft. 6 in.
Girders 6 in. x 6 in.
First floor joists 2 in. x 8 in.
Ceiling joists 2 in. x 4 in. Rafters 2 in. x 4 in.
Front door—our "Saranac," design, 3 ft. x 6 ft.
    8 in. and 1¾ in. thick, glazed. *See pages 36–37.*
Our kitchen cupboard No. 2 included in the selling
    price. *See pages 36–37.*

PLAN B—
Ceiling height first floor approximately 8 ft. 6 in.
Girders 6 in. x 6 in.
First floor joists 2 in. x 8 in.
Ceiling joists 2 in. x 4 in. Rafters 2 in. x 4 in.
Front door—our "Saranac," design, 3 ft. x 6 ft.
    8 in. and 1¾ in. thick. *See pages 36–37.*
Our kitchen cupboard No. 2 and medicine cabinet
    included in the selling price. *See pages 36–37.*

See pages 8–9 for general specifications.

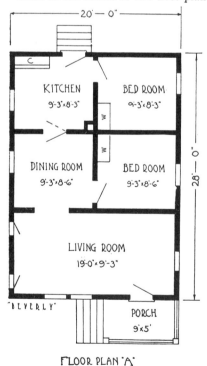

FLOOR PLAN "A"

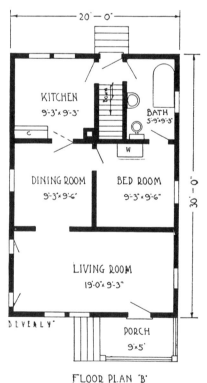

FLOOR PLAN "B"

Concord

**20 ft. x 30 ft. or
22 ft. x 30 ft. over all
5 Rooms and Bath**

Beyond the rather striking economy which we believe you find in purchasing your home the Bennett-Way, there is considerable increased worth both in the appearance and in the quality of material that we send you to put into your home—the Concord is fully up to Bennett standards. To its rather simple proportions has been added an overhanging, bracketed roof, and a snug porch.

The pattern of the window sash and frames and the shingled sides also add their bit to this comfortable looking little home. The floor plan itself speaks for the interior of the home. But let's call your particular attention to the rather generous closet space off both bedrooms, the well-lighted and well-aired rooms, the convenient kitchen cabinet—all contained in the modest proportions of 20 ft. by 30 ft.

We believe the selling price of the Concord is quite in keeping with the most efficient home economy ideas. Certain it is that from other owner's experiences, we can guarantee enduring and entire satisfaction with the Concord, if it is your choice.

SPECIFICATIONS

Ceiling height first floor approximately 9 ft.
Girders 6 in. x 6 in.
First floor joists 2 in. x 8 in.
Ceiling joists 2 in. x 4 in.   Rafters 2 in. x 4 in.
Front door—cottage design, 2 ft. 8 in. x 6 ft. 8 in.
   and 1¾ in. thick, glazed. *See pages 36–37.*
Our kitchen cupboard No. 2 included in the selling
   price. *See pages 36–37.*
Our kitchen cupboard No. 1 and Niagara Colonnade
   included in selling price of Plan B.

See pages 8–9 for general specifications.

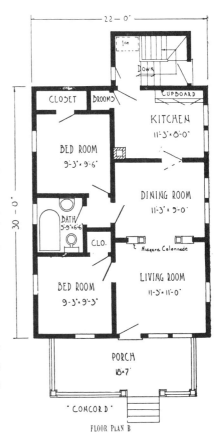

FLOOR PLAN "CONCORD"

FLOOR PLAN B

61

Emerson

**24 ft. x 32 ft. over all
5 Rooms and Bath**

This is an extremely neat and inexpensive home to build, easy to keep in order, easy to heat and make comfortable. The porch across the front will be a great comfort in summer, and at little expense it may be screened and converted into a comfortable out-of-door room.

The vestibule will help keep out the cold of winter, and the adjoining coat closet provides a splendid place for wraps and rubbers. The living room is large and comfortable. The wide-cased opening leading from the dining room gives it an effect of still greater proportion and the dining room is also attractive with its grouped windows. The interior hall arrangement provides easy access to bath and bedrooms. The well-lighted kitchen is of convenient size and is particu-

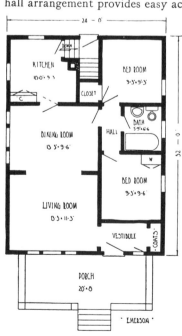

FLOOR PLAN

larly pleasing, providing a light, cheery, comfortable room within easy access of the dining room. The cellar entrance at grade, you will find another desirable feature.

The ownership of the Emerson will prove a never-ending source of satisfaction and content.

SPECIFICATIONS

Ceiling height first floor approximately 9 ft.

Girders 6 in. x 8 in.

First floor joists 2 in. x 8 in.

Ceiling joists 2 in. x 4 in. Rafters 2 in. x 4 in.

Front door—our "Chautauqua" of solid Chestnut, 3 ft. x 6 ft. 8 in. and 1¾ in. thick, glazed with clear glass.

Our No. 2 kitchen cupboard and medicine cabinet included in selling price. *See pages 36–37.*

See pages 8–9 for general specifications.

FEW INDIVIDUALS WHO DESIGN THEIR OWN HOMES KNOW HOW TO ARRIVE AT THE COST OF MATERIAL AND LABOR.

Hopewell Junction, N. Y.
May 20, 1919.

Gentlemen:—

The building material shipped me came in good condition, was of good grade which rather *surprised* some of our *old carpenters*, it being much better quality than they have been using. I hope to build another house as soon as this one is finished, and shall remember you with the order.

Sincerely,
J. L. F.

Waverly

24 ft. x 38 ft. over all
5 Rooms and Bath

The beauty and charm of this comfortable bungalow are instantly appreciated by every true home lover. It is a masterpiece in bungalow architecture. See the low sloped roof, wide bracketed eaves, grouped windows, built-up rail, shingled side walls, a true California bungalow and a favorite in that country which has become a model for all the world. The front porch is an unusually pretty feature. What an attractive departure the balusters and timbered effect are from the usual combination of rail and balusters. The bay window is just what is needed to break up the wall space and adds greatly to the general pleasing effect. Picture this bungalow on your lot, side walls stained a light seal brown, moss green for the roof, with pure white trimming, shrubbery nestled along the front and corners of the porch. Wouldn't you be proud to say "This is my home"? Often an attractive exterior will be found to conceal a poor arrangement of rooms. This is not the case with the Waverly. Careful attention has been given to details and we believe that every housewife will appreciate the excellent floor plan arrangement. You enter direct from the porch into one of the prettiest living rooms you have ever seen. Triple windows in front and side are among the attractive features of this room, allowing worlds of sunshine and cheer to enter, but still leaving plenty of wall space for furniture. The high casement windows in the end were separated purposely to provide a place for your piano. The well-lighted dining room is separated from the living room by an attractive colonnade-arch. The kitchen is conveniently located for serving and for easy access to the grade cellar entrance. Bedrooms and bath open into an interior hall which makes these private but within easy access of all rooms. We are sure that the Waverly will meet your highest expectations.

SPECIFICATIONS

Ceiling height first floor approximately 9 ft.
Girders 6 in. x 8 in.
Ceiling joists 2 in. x 4 in. Rafters 2 in. x 4 in.
Front door—our "Conesus," of solid Chestnut, 3 ft.
    x 6 ft. 8 in. and 1¾ in. thick, glazed with
    clear glass.
Niagara colonnade between living room and dining
    room. *See pages 36–37.*
Our kitchen cupboard No. 2, wardrobes and medi-
    cine cabinet included in the selling price. *See*
    pages 36–37.

See pages 8–9 for general specifications.

MORE THAN SATISFIED

Olean, N. Y.
December 28, 1919.

Gentlemen:—

    Be assured we shall not forget you whenever we may have occasion to mention or suggest ready-cut houses, for our Erie is more than satisfactory.

        N. E. P.

Ontario

26 ft. x 34 ft. over all
5 Rooms and Bath

Can you imagine a more pleasing and homelike design than the Ontario at such a moderate cost? Great care was used to secure this attractive, harmonious exterior and still retain the exceptionally convenient and practical arrangement of rooms. The front porch with its large tapering columns, wide overhanging bracketed eaves and roof dormer at side, all serve to give this design a distinct individuality. The vestibule and coat closet will be found a desirable arrangement. The living room and dining room are made especially attractive with triple windows, having an extra wide cased opening between the living room and the dining room, making this practically one room—a feature desired by many. The kitchen is of a convenient size and well lighted. Our kitchen cupboard No. 2 is a part of the finish in this room and is supplied as a part of the equipment. The grade entrance is another added convenience. A large storage space is provided for in the attic, attic stairs and flooring being included in the selling price. Bedrooms are of good size with large closet-space. The interior hall arrangement provides easy access to bath and bedrooms. If you are looking for comfort and a home of which you may be proud, select the Ontario

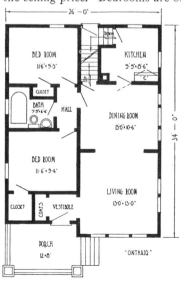

FLOOR PLAN

SPECIFICATIONS

Ceiling height first floor approximately 9 ft.

Girders 6 in. x 8 in.

First floor joists 2 in. x 8 in.

Second floor joists 2 in. x 6 in.

Rafters 2 in. x 6 in.

Front door—our "Mohawk," of solid Chestnut, 3 ft. x 6 ft. 8 in. 1¾ in. thick, glazed with clear glass. *See pages 36–37.*

Our No. 2 kitchen cupboard and medicine cabinet included in the selling price. *See pages 36–37*

Attic stairs and flooring included in selling price.

See pages 8–9 for general specificattions.

PROMPT AND EFFICIENT SERVICE

Richmondville, N. Y.

December 27, 1919.

Gentlemen:—

I desire to thank you for the prompt and efficient service which you have given me and for the prompt attention which has been given to all of my orders and assure you that if I can do any good in this section, I will gladly do it.

My new home is nearly completed and as soon as the lawn is graded and some shrubbery placed, in the spring, I will send you a picture of same.

C. A. B.

Stanley

26 ft. x 20 ft. over all
4 Rooms

To combine attractiveness, individuality and economy in one design requires skill, but you will find that the Stanley possesses them all. A more attractive cottage could hardly be imagined. You can see that the pretty exterior effect is obtained by the use of a well proportioned porch, large built-up porch columns, broad overhanging roof, clapboards for side walls with shingles and panels for gables. One of our most attractive front doors, the "Conesus," and the latest style of panel sash are furnished with this design.

The living room, bedrooms and kitchen are expertly arranged to secure the greatest amount of comfort and convenience. If a basement is desired, an enclosed cellar addition may be added at rear in place of the stoop, at small cost. Notice that each room has two windows, thus insuring perfect ventilation.

Two roomy closets give ample space for clothes. Either living room or kitchen is sufficiently large to be used also as a dining room.

On the whole this cottage is altogether charming and will strongly appeal to those who desire a modern four-room house but whose purse places a limit on the amount to be expended.

SPECIFICATIONS

Ceiling height first floor approximately 9 ft.

Girders 6 in. x 6 in.

First floor joists 2 in. x 8 in.

Ceiling joists 2 in. x 4 in. Rafters 2 in. x 4 in.

Front door—our "Conesus," of solid Chestnut, 3 ft. x 6 ft. 8 in. and 1¾ in. thick, glazed with clear glass. *See pages 36–37.*

Our No. 2 kitchen cupboard included in selling price. *See pages 36–37.*

See pages 8–9 for general specifications

FLOOR PLAN

GOES TOGETHER LIKE A CHARM

Norfolk, Va.
December 17, 1919.

Gentlemen:—

Please send catalogue to enclosed list. These people are all thinking of building and have shown great interest in my Ilion.

From the favorable comments I hear concerning my house you should be able to stir up some business here.

I am making good progress with my house. The stuff goes together like a charm.

L. M. K.

(Note: His Ilion proved so eminently satisfactory that he has since placed an order for the Potomac.)

Madison

24 ft. x 28 ft. over all
8 Rooms and Bath

The Madison is planned to meet the requirements for a square house that can be built on a lot of medium size and still give comfortably large rooms. Notice how well the rooms are arranged to utilize every inch of space. This hospitable front porch will be appreciated during the summer when at a little expense, it may be screened and converted into a comfortable out-of-door room. The enclosed porch balustrade with its added seclusion is a very desirable feature in a house set close to the street.

The reception hall in this home is an unusually attractive and cozy apartment with its broad staircase and pretty landing. A wide-cased arch leads into the comfortable living room. It is not necessary to crowd your furniture in this room or set it at an angle, for there is plenty of wall space for the largest pieces. You will like the beautiful, well-lighted dining room with its built-in window-seat and grouped windows. See how nicely you can arrange your buffet, serving table and china cabinet and still have plenty of wall space for chairs.

Every housewife will appreciate the thought we have given in designing the kitchen. See how conveniently you can arrange your equipment to save unnecessary steps. The range at the inside wall, the sink and work tables in front of windows, your large kitchen cabinet placed just right. Notice the convenience in the icebox arrangement, only a step or two from the kitchen, still out of the way and iced without going into the kitchen. The arrangement of rooms on the second floor is ideal. The bedrooms are large and well lighted with plenty of closet space. The bath is within easy reach of all bedrooms as well as the stairs.

SPECIFICATIONS

Ceiling height first floor approximately 9 ft.
Ceiling height second floor approximately 8 ft.
Girders 6 in. x 8 in.
First and second floor joists 2 in. x 8 in.
Ceiling joists 2 in. x 4 in. Rafters 2 in. x 6 in.
Front door—our "Conesus," of solid Chestnut, 3 ft. x 6 ft. 8 in.
 and 1¾ in. thick, glazed with clear glass. *See pages 36–37.*
Our No. 1 kitchen cupboard, wardrobes and medicine cabinet
 included in the selling price of this house. *See pages 36–37.*

See pages 8–9 for general specifications.

66

Tremont

32 ft. x 34 ft. over all
Twin House
6 Rooms and Bath—Each

To meet the present and constantly increasing demand for a practical twin house that can be erected on an average city lot, we present this attractive design. From the exterior, one would never even suspect that this house contained two complete suites of rooms.

The vestibule divides the porch so that each family has its own private porch. From the large, well-lighted living room, separated by a wide cased arch is the attractive dining room.

Notice the convenient coat closet, a very essential feature in every home.

The kitchen is very conveniently located for serving. The built-in cupboards and shelves extend the full width. The entry-way provides space for the refrigerator, brooms, etc. On the second floor, you have three nice bedrooms, each one provided with wardrobes. The bath is conveniently located at the end of the hall within easy access of chambers and stairs. A large, well-lighted attic and attic stairs have also been provided for with floor and partition dividing the attic which are also included in the price of this house.

The Tremont offers an excellent investment, rental income doubled. The proportional greater cost over a single house is insignificant when compared with the net profit.

SPECIFICATIONS

Ceiling height first floor approximately 9 ft.
Ceiling height second floor approximately 8 ft.
Girders 6 in. x 8 in.
First and second floor joists 2 in. x 8 in.
Ceiling joists 2 in. x 6 in.
Rafters 2 in. x 6 in.
Front door—our "Chautauqua," of solid Chestnut, 3 ft. x 6 ft. 8 in. and 1¾ in. thick, glazed with clear glass. *See pages 36–37.*
Oak floors and trim for living room and dining room quoted on application. Special kitchen cupboard, wardrobes and medicine cabinet included in the selling price. *See pages 36–37.*

See pages 8-9 for general specifications.

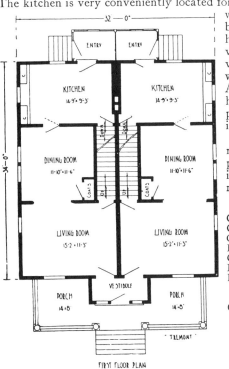

FIRST FLOOR PLAN

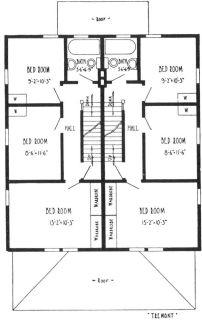

SECOND FLOOR PLAN

GENERAL SPECIFICATIONS FOR BENNETT SUMMER COTTAGES

Cedar posts for two foot grade.

Foundation sills—4 x 6 in. No. 1 Hemlock, cut to fit.

Floor joists—2 x 6 in. No. 1 Hemlock, cut to fit, spaced 2 ft. O. C.

Studding—2 x 4 in. No. 1 Hemlock, dressed four sides, cut to fit, spaced 2 ft. O. C. Walls 8 ft. high.

Rafters—2 x 4 in. No. 1 Hemlock, dressed four sides, cut to fit, spaced 2 ft. O. C.

Wall ties—2 x 4 in. No. 1 Hemlock, dressed four sides, cut to fit.

Wainscoting—Dressed, matched and beaded, 2 ft. high, where shown in illustration, cut to fit.

Siding—1 x 6 in. Fir novelty siding, tongued and grooved, dressed both sides, cut to fit.

Roof Sheathing—1 x 6 in. No. 1 Hemlock, dressed and matched, cut to fit.

Roof Covering—Bennett 3-ply prepared roofing, or extra *A* Red Cedar Shingles, if preferred.

Exterior Finish—White Pine, cut to fit.

Flooring—1 x 4 in. Yellow Pine or Fir, dressed and matched, cut to fit.

Partitions—1 x 4 in. No. 1 Ceiling, dressed and matched and beaded both sides, cut to fit. Partitions 7 ft. high. (The rooms are all open to rafters.)

Doors and windows glazed as shown in illustrations. (Interior doors furnished where shown in plans.)

Interior door and window trim—1 x 3 in. Yellow Pine.

Paint for two good coats outside, including the porch floor and steps, any color. (Color card mailed upon request.)

Hardware, nails, locks, hinges.

No paints, stains or varnishes furnished for interior.

No masonry, lath, plaster or plaster board furnished.

Screens, storm doors and storm windows not included—prices quoted on application.

Stoops and steps included when shown in plans, cut to fit.

Reversed plans will be furnished without extra cost.

Bennett Summer Cottages are designed with the same care as Bennett Homes. The lumber and mill work furnished throughout is the same high grade as used with our best houses.

WENONA

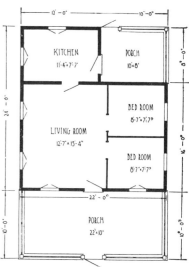

" WENONA "

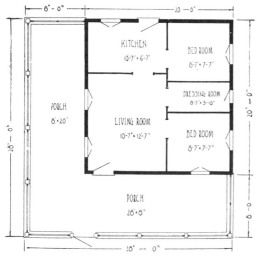

" NEWPORT "

NEWPORT

IVERNIA

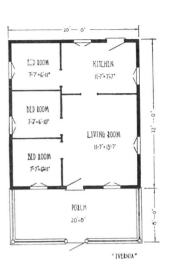

"IVERNIA"

We Guarantee Entire Satisfaction or Money Back

We guarantee to furnish all lumber, shingles, finishing lumber, doors, windows, frames, floor and interior trim, hardware, nails, paints of sufficient quantity and equal to or better than the grades specified, to complete the house according to the plans and specifications on opposite page. We further guarantee that there will be no extras, and that all material will reach you in perfect condition. Should any shortages occur, we agree to replace the material either by shipping the necessary material or paying you whatever it costs to buy locally.

"LINWOOD"

LINWOOD

All of the material in these cottages comes to you completely ready-cut, every piece plainly marked. Plans and instructions are so simple and easily understood, that they can be erected in from three to five days by unskilled labor.

Every piece of material is guaranteed accurately cut to fit.

Specifications for Bennett Special Garage

Studding—2 x 4 in. No. 1 Hemlock, spaced 36 O. C. cut to fit.

Circular Rafters cut from 2 x 12 in. No. 1 Hemlock, cut to fit.

Siding—1 x 6 in. Fir novelty siding, dressed and matched, cut to fit.

Hardware—All necessary hardware and nails included in selling price.

Roof Sheathing—1 x 6 in. No. 1 Hemlock, dressed and matched, cut to fit.

Roof Covering—Bennett 3-ply roofing.

Doors—1 x 4 in. Ceiling, cut to fit.

Paint—Two coats paint for outside.

Floor—No material for floor is furnished. If such is desired, we will, upon request, gladly quote prices.

THE BENNETT SPECIAL

BENNETT SPECIAL GARAGE

HUDSON—Touring Car Size

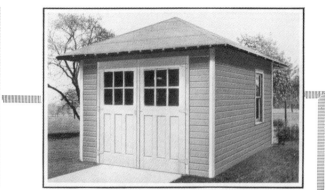

BUICK—Roadster or Medium Size

PEERLESS—Double Large-Car Size

CADILLAC—Double Large-Car Size

GARAGES

Up to the Bennett Better-Built standard in every item, yet low priced. Very quickly erected. Well lighted, snug, substantial. Liberal space for cars, with working room aplenty at sides.

SPECIFICATIONS

STUDDING: 2 in. x 4 in. No. 1 Hemlock, spaced 24 in. on centers. Cut to fit.
RAFTERS: 2 in. x 4 in. No. 1 Hemlock, spaced 24 in. on centers, surfaced 4 sides. Cut to fit.
SIDING: 1 in. x 6 in. Clear Fir Novelty. Cut to fit.
ROOF SHEATHING: See individual specifications.
HARDWARE: All necessary hardware and nails included in selling price.
FLOOR: No material for floor is furnished. If such is desired, we will upon request, gladly quote prices.

WALL PLATES: 2 in. x 4 in. No. 1 Hemlock, double at top, single at bottom of studding. Cut to fit.
ROOF COVERING: See individual specifications.
DOORS: As shown in illustration. Glazed opening 8 in. x 8 in.
WINDOWS: See individual specifications.
PAINT: Sufficient quantity of Bennett House Paint for two good coats. colors as specified by purchaser.

BUICK

ROOF SHEATHING: 1 in. x 6 in. No. 1 Hemlock, dressed, matched and cut to fit.
ROOF COVERING: Asphalt Slate-Surfaced Roll-Roofing. Shingles will

be furnished at a slight additional cost, if desired.
WINDOWS: Two sliding sash windows and frames, 26 in. x 26 in. glazed. For various sizes see price list.

HUDSON

ROOF SHEATHING: 1 in. x 4 in. No. 1 Hemlock, spaced 2¼ in. apart. Cut to fit.
WINDOWS: Three 3-light sash and frames, each light 10 in. x 20 in., glazed.

ROOF COVERING: Extra Clear Red Cedar Shingles, laid 4½ in. to the weather.
For various sizes see price list.

PEERLESS

ROOF SHEATHING: 1 in. x 4 in. No. 1 Hemlock, spaced 2½ in. apart. Cut to fit.
ROOF COVERING: Extra Clear Red Cedar Shingles, laid 4½ in. to the weather.

WINDOWS: Three 3-light sash and frames, each light 10 in. x 20 in. glazed.
SIDE DOOR: 2 ft. 8 in. x 6 ft. 8 in. mortised for lock set. For various sizes see price list.

CADILLAC

ROOF SHEATHING: 1 in. x 4 in. No. 1 Hemlock, spaced 2¼ in. apart. Cut to fit.
WINDOWS: Three 3-light sash and frames, each light 10 in. x 20 in., glazed.

ROOF COVERING: Extra Clear Red Cedar shingles, laid 4½ in. to the weather.
For various sizes see price list.

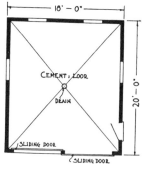

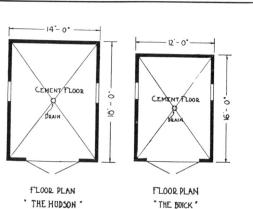

FLOOR PLAN
"THE CADILLAC"

FLOOR PLAN
"THE PEERLESS"

FLOOR PLAN
"THE HUDSON"

FLOOR PLAN
"THE BUICK"

MODERN EQUIPMENT FOR YOUR HOME

Bennett Plumbing Fixtures

A BATHROOM LIKE THIS WILL BE A CREDIT TO YOUR HOME

The Home Equipment Book offers a variety of high grade, attractive fixtures to choose from.

Be sure to get this book.

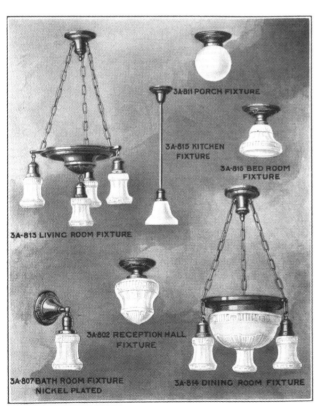

3A-811 PORCH FIXTURE

3A-815 KITCHEN FIXTURE

3A-815 BED ROOM FIXTURE

3A-813 LIVING ROOM FIXTURE

3A-802 RECEPTION HALL FIXTURE

3A-807 BATH ROOM FIXTURE NICKEL PLATED

3A-814 DINING ROOM FIXTURE

Bennett Pipeless Furnace

Cold weather comfort and convenience. Costs little more than a stove.

Heats the entire house with one register. Warm air is forced to all rooms and cold air is drawn off the floors.

Requires little attention. Burns any kind of fuel. Hard or soft coal, coke or wood.

Easy to install. A man and a boy can set it up in a single day.

No need to cut up your floors and walls.

Economical in fuel. Heats up quickly.

No heat wasted in the basement. Keeps cellar cool for fruits and vegetables.

For sizes and prices see HOME EQUIPMENT BOOK.

HOME EQUIPMENT BOOK

A Guide For the Home Owner. It Will Help You Equip Your New Home With Modern Conveniences at a Saving.

Send For Your Copy Today

RAY H. BENNETT LUMBER CO., INC.

Bennett Home Equipment Service
Puts the Finishing Touch on Home Comfort

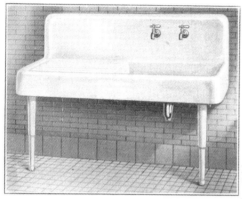

KITCHEN SINK

An attractive sink, massive in construction, cast in one solid piece from best grade of gray iron and heavily white enameled. All corners are rounded to prevent accumulation of grease and dirt. Deep rim hides entire painted bottom of sink. Furnished with drain board on either right or left hand side. Length, 52 inches over all. Size of sink, 20 x 28 inches. *See Home Equipment Book for other styles and sizes.*

LAUNDRY STOVE

Combination laundry stove and heater. Heats laundry room and supplies hot water for domestic use. Has flat oval top plate, 16 in. wide. and 25½ in. long. Will accommodate a wash boiler or six flatirons. Has durable grate with draw center. Water jacket surrounds entire firepot. Has capacity for heating 60 gallons of water. *See Home Equipment Book for price.*

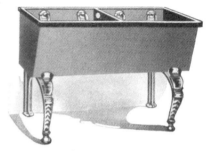

LAUNDRY TUB

Two-compartment laundry tub made from best grade of imported Portland cement and crushed granite. Moulded in one solid piece. Inside corners are nicely rounded so tub can be easily kept clean. Top edges are fitted with patent metallic rim and wringer guard. *See Home Equipment Book for other sizes.*

A kerosene heater which is absolutely efficient. Heats just as well as gas. Has double copper coils. Patented burner. No wicks. Heats water quickly and economically. Complete with kerosene tank of one gallon capacity. *See Home Equipment Book.*

KEROSENE WATER HEATER

RANGE BOILER

Galvanized range boiler for storing hot water under pressure. Connected to water front in the kitchen stove or to a coil in the furnace, or heated by water heater. Insures a constant supply of warm water for domestic use. Furnished in 30, 40 or 52 gallon sizes. *See Home Equipment Book.*

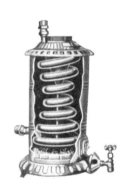

Efficient gas burning water heater with black sheet steel casing. Water runs through double copper coil and is heated by large burner shown at bottom. Conical shape of coil provides maximum heating efficiency. Suitable for heating 30 gallon range boiler. *See Home Equipment Book for larger heaters.*

WARM AIR FURNACE

Heating, Plumbing, Lighting Service—Free

Modern heating, sanitary plumbing and electric lighting are essential to home contentment. Let our service department solve your equipment problems without placing you under any obligations. Our experts will gladly give you reliable advice on every point.

You will find our Home Equipment Book an interesting guide in selecting fixtures to suit your taste.

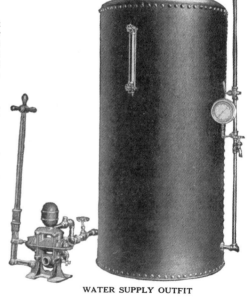

WATER SUPPLY OUTFIT

BAKER, JONES, HAUSAUER, INC., PRINTERS
BUFFALO, N. Y.

Interior Decorating
SERVICE FREE

SOMETIME ago the thought came to us:
"We build our Bennett Homes soundly and artistically on the outside and inside. We use the finest trained talent in the country to give our home-builders the very best to be had in architecture and workmanship. Why not assist our home-keepers in selecting and arranging the furnishings of those homes?"

Every woman wants her home to express charm, personality, good taste. But every woman does not care to employ a high-priced interior decorator. Yet it must be conceded that someone who does nothing all day but plan colors, lights and furniture arrangement, can save, through wide experience, long days and nights of anxious thought for the home-keeper. To get just the prettiest arrangement for rooms really does take much valuable time and much trouble.

So we have taken into our Organization two women advisers for our home-keepers. These women are expert interior decorators who do nothing but plan for our Homes Beautiful. It does not matter whether your home and the amount of money you wish to spend be small or large—our experts will help you plan to the very best advantage with whatever you care to spend. Too, they will either plan entirely, or help you plan—as you choose. They know, thoroughly, every home that we build—every nook and corner of every one of them. They have furnished some many times over—every time differently. If you wish merely suggestions as to various color schemes in walls, floors, hangings, or if you wish to use furniture you already have, but in a new way—or if you desire to furnish your homes entirely, down to the last detail of picture hanging and effective plant-placing, they are glad and willing to answer any and every question and to give all advice in their power.

An especial feature of their service is helping you plan your kitchen efficiently, according to modern methods of steps and energy saving. They have planned many hundreds of model kitchens and can help you stock and arrange yours so that you will save time from drudgery of routine, for the enjoyment of a book, the good outdoors, or your social life.

[Original back cover]